BOB & DAVE

'Teesside... If the boot fits'

Facebook.com/warcrypublishing
Dave Taylor / Jamie Boyle (c)

NOTE:

The views and opinions expressed in this book are those of the interviewees obtained during recorded interview and do not necessarily reflect the opinions of the author.

Bob & Dave: 'Teesside... If the boot fits'

ISBN: 978-1-912543-33-5

Cover Design: Gavin Parker UK

Printed and bound in Great Britain by PMM Goup Ltd, UK.

Find out more at: facebook.com/warcrypublishing

This book is a tribute to a true legend, Frankie W Taylor April 1966 - March 2000. My brother, my best friend, my hero. He was with me every step of the way, I know he will be looking down laughing and bursting with pride. I was then, I still am, and I always will be proud of you kid. R.I.P Frankie XX

Your little brother... Dave

Contents

"Every day that I keep Bob out of jail is a good day."

Dave

Foreword

JAMIE BOYLE
– AUTHOR / FILM MAKER

Where do I start with the legends that areBob & Dave? I suppose I'll start by saying this two-man mobis my gift to the world.I've been writing books for almost three years now, I've been told I've captured the iconic Lee Duffy to a tee by the thousands of readers, particularly the ones who knew Lee at close quarters but I haven't only written about the Teesside names, I've tackled the national names such as Paul Sykes, Roy Shaw and Dominic Negus.

Now, I know you'rewondering how I stumbled across a couple of fully-fledged loons like Bob & Dave? Well, the truth is I've always liked comedy and it's a BIG part of my personality. Anybody who knows Jamie Boyle at well will tell you I'm a right eefing oddball(but in the nicest possible way of course). Writing books and making documentaries is only 50% of my job because the other 50% is dealing with sales. There's no point writing the world's best books if you don't advertise them so I've been using social media a fair amount and this is where I came across these two fine young gentlemen of Teesside.

Over a period of maybe a year or so I had watched the videos of these two guys in the gym dressed head to toe,usually in Slazenger, you'd have thought these two funny fuckers were sponsored by Sports Direct. The videos always ended up with the big bald one threatening someone whilst the other one would be trying to talk somesense into the angry one. After several months I think I must have friend requested Robert Prosser and Dave Taylor on

Facebook and then I got talking to Dave whowas mulling over putting togetherthe adventures of Bob & Dave in a book. When Dave told me this I was all ears and I offered him a contract there and then. This book is the result!

In my opinion, everybody needs a little humour in their lives and this is what Bob & Dave bring to Teesside. The fact of the matter is that these two don't take themselves too seriously at all and for that reason, I think they're brilliant. They're just two middle-aged men who've refused to grow up and, I'm told, there's always fun and laughter every single time these two colossal units train in Steel City gym, for free of course because the owners are too scared to charge them.

Ladies and gentlemen, I give you my gift to the world Bob & Dave: 'Teesside... If The Boot Fits' is a story of two young men, one from Thorntree, the other from Normanby and how they became to own the town of Middlesbrough and everything in it. The myth, the legend and the folklore stories will be embedded in Teesside history fifty years from now and all your grandchildren will know the names of Bob & Dave. Please believe me though folks, whatever you've heard about them on the criminal grapevine their actual story is far scarier. Lee Duffy used to stand all night opening doors for Bob in the Blues, Brian Cockerill made himself a recluse and the all-time hide and seek champion for over a decade because he owed Dave a score, Viv Graham put himself in jail to escape the gruesome pair in 1989 and Terry Dicko's illegal nightclub The Steampacket only closed in 2003 on Bob's orders, not Cleveland police's orders as its largely believed.There are some book books which I've been involved with which have turned out to have been a right bore, this book I'd have been involved for free because it has been a pleasure to have been involved with Bob & Dave and their journey so far. Plus the fact they'd kick the shit out of me if I didn't publish their story. As I'm typing this the brains behind the operation Dave is already planning to write the sequel and we've even spoken about a comedy documentary.

From myself and Warcry Publications we give you, Bob & Dave – If The Boot Fits… ENJOY.

P.S. For those of you not familiar with the Teesside lingo, get yourselves on YouTube, learn our dialect (it's the best in the country), sort your life out and have a Parmo! You'll never look back!

Introduction

Teesside, I will leave you with that word for a moment to summon whatever thoughts or feelings it may. Does it bring about anything special, or has it conjured old feelings of dread and despair? For some, it may be steel and ships, for others that sense of community whereby doors were unlocked and people talked shit over a brew, for many it will be the hills and scramblers carving new tracks in the land on a weekend whilst being chased by the law, or some shit bag from south bank who wants your bike. Is it the big blue bridge the world famous, affectionately named 'the transporter', motionless, standing there staring at the town with cold eyes, and legs spread like a cheap punk who has been turned away from the club?For some, it's the murky river tees and the ghosts that it keeps as a secret, or maybe it's endless indoor farms that litter the estates, professionally constructed to churn out the greener things in life.For some, it's the chemical plants spewing smog into the air we breathe, built like entire cities across the land turning it into a giant laboratory, or maybe it's that white powder that abundantly floods the nightlife by insomniacs, that is dropped off like a pizza delivery through the night to shit conversations in the kitchen. Teesside, with its own language an all tha, that takes a week to master and a lifetime to understand, for some it's Ravanelli and Juninho, or kicki ball spyo, knockyknockyhido, or some other game that always got you a chase from the homeowner. Or is it the much more sinister and unpleasant shady underworld, cram packed with unsavoury characters, whose reputations have completely been constructed from the Chinese whispers, by shit bags, hangers-on and soldiers who translate half told stories of miss matched street fights, and heroic lies cooked up to gain attention in the social club, on a dust fuelled Sunday afternoon?This is where the invisible warriors are created, it's where a man can become king and ruler in one conversation, and never really have to lift a finger or have any knowledge of the event. It may be the blue giro collecting storytellers of yesteryear that tell a cracking tail, dropping names like bombs over Germany, and with their own touch of seasoning. Or it maybe the cloned ladies straight off the production line all looking the same, with wood shavings for hair and 5 ml holding their faces together, because here in Teesside we have more make-up artists per square inch than New York. For some it's the "their kids are their world" posts on social media, except on a weekend when the dads are supposed to step up but never do, making for a Facebook status on Monday morning, over a cuppa with Shelly, or Janet, or is it the folk law gospel word of St Belcher Chain that says, you can't fuck with "skegzo" because he's sort of a gypsy, or don't cross words with billy bob because his dad once had a fight with mad bonka!You see this is how it all works, misjudged verbal reputations get somehow confused with capable tough guys that say nothing, and just get on with their lives. Don't forget the hardest man in any town probably sits and watches television every night with his children. For me it's the real people, the very few that still know how to spell loyalty, the handful of warriors that can tell a true story without seasoning, these people grab your attention because you know the tail is unflavoured, this lot that are made of stuff you can longer buy, these folks are the ones that take a jail sentence without committing a crime for a pal, just because it's an unspoken language. I know this lot, and as uncouth as they may seem you're always in safe hands, we are from this stock, pedigree's that would win best in show if there was such a thing. Maybe it's the nightlife, the unlicensed tracksuit wearing doorman with the unofficial title like, "beverage manager" lingering around the club front door like he's some sort of troubleshooter, who only really has the job because he's a complete head the ball. But it's not all bad, there are some great people in this backward place, people that would give you their last and hide you in the loft from the law if need be, doors always open and kettles always on, New Year's Eve front doors wide open to any cunt that wants a cocktail stick, with a hotdog, pickled onion and a cube of cheese attached to it. There was always a sense of belonging in Teesside, everyone's mother always called you son, and would always say things like "tell ya mam I was asking", and you could borrow anything from milk to a shit roll, without fear of judgment because we're all in the same boat. The Teesside times, that rag that was unreadable and that was never ever delivered, by that shite paperboy who was wider than the river, it would always end up in the big silver bins somewhere at the back of a block of flats.

Like anywhere else there are germs, and germs multiply, so whether it's the bent police officers that run around like some sort of 'no rules apply' mobsters, trading drugs for information, or else, controlled by even more corrupt inspectors, that occasionally put on a stab vest and take part in raids, just to earn cute little titles like Robocop to climb their own crooked ladder or agenda, or is it a particular pub, there are so many shitholes that carry stories of humour, war and deceit. I have mine and I have fond memories. You see in our place you could, at one time, buy just about anything from clothes to "I swear down dead it's real " MOT certificates, or it just might be the hundreds of 'you're fooling nobody' small businesses fronted by the dinosaur wide boy that is clinging to power an all tha. Fag sellers a plenty with swallow tattooed hands and leather skin given to them by the sun that lives in Benidorm, yeah they used to be rock hard too. So, I want you to relate to our world and connect with this story in some way, emotionally or other. I have to say that the place is unique.

Whatever the word 'Teesside' brings up for you is yours, own it. We are about to take you through the layers of this place, to parts you don't see, the tasteless and bittersweet characters that lurk in the foundations of the place we call Teesside. This is the story of the infamous taxmen of taxmen, where it all began, through the sociopathic minds of the ones they dare to call Bob and Dave. So ladies and gentlemen, "If the boot fits".

"Ere….. I wanna grand off ya!"

Bob

1

Bob's World

The world of Bob and Dave is not for the young or old, nor would the weak survive in this hidden part of the matrix, that you only see if you play the game, the game being money, and power. Bob and Dave were no strangers to the underworld, I might add at this stage Bob is the underworld, like the Greek god Hades he is the king of the place. He moves around as obviously as you would imagine, bolshie and loud, he's not careful, he's not forgiving or kind, he is how they say "oh contraire to normality", he bumbles around the place with presence, eye contact gets you a "fuck you looking at?" Being in the same room gets you a "al punch your fucking head in." You see if you want to survive in Bob's world you need to pin back your ears and listen up, you need to stand to attention and remain still, and even Dave knows the drill by now.

Bob is clumsy and unapologetic, even when an apology is required, he replaces the word "sorry" with something a little straighter forward like "so fuck", and that was if he liked you a tiny bit. If you exist in Bob's world, it is because he wants you in it not because he likes you, or because you have courageously said "hello" under your breath as you passed him in the gym, but because Bob thinks you're an asset, an asset he can use in the future and dispose of like a shitty nappy an all tha, so beware.

If you ever find yourself in Bob's company and unscathed and free from fear you should maybe ask yourself "why am I here?" Bob essentially lives his life for very few things, money, power, the gym, and to punch the fuck out of anyone that so much as challenges this entitlement, and that means anyone.

When your wardrobe consists of a range of XXXL Slazenger vests and jogger bottoms you mean business, always ready to go and always game as fuck, always ready to go to the town and smash up doorman five at a time, wearing boxing boots and the infamous vest.It's not personal,Bob has a reputation to keep up, and a bare knuckle down the town is as good as any to start the Chinese whispers, but the whispers won't need that extra shitbag seasoning that usually gets sprinkled as the story gets passed around, there will only ever be one version of anything Bob gets involved in, whether its a door takeover, a tax on a local drug Lord, or Bob just wanting this hell hole to know he's still around by bashing three or four bullies at once.See bob would always insist they go get their pals before handing out discipline, and I am always glued to his back in these situations even though it's against the way I operate, Bob is my brother, my pal, my right hand and that is priceless in a town we're relationships with the law are, let's say a little inappropriate if you get what I mean.

Bob and the law should not be spoken of in the same sentence, but they often are when they provide him an all-inclusive holiday once in a while. Bob didn't mind a trip away now n then he had his own room, when he arrived they would club together and put a spread on an all tha, even the screws would chip in. It was always a sad time for me to see him go, if I wasn't going with him, which did happen now and then. This always left me feeling a little vulnerable, our castle would have less defence but this was where the brains came in useful, I would keep my ear to the ground, listening out for easy pickings, and fruits that were very much in season for when the big man came home. Let's not forget, Teesside was Bob's and Bob was Teesside.

"LET COCKERILL GET HIS FIVE MINS OF FAME OFF OUR NAMES. BRIAN KNOWS I COULD STAMP HIM OUT LIKE A ROLLY IF I WANTED TOO".

DAVE

Who is Dave?

Now, where does Dave fit into all this?Well some say that Dave is like the shadow, he is always there but rarely seen, he is the diary, the secretary, the real brain behind the outfit, some say he created Bob, much like Frankenstein in a lab with nuts, bolts, and electricity, stolen, of course, from next door but this cannot be confirmed an all tha, He is the calm before the storm. In all of the madness, it is he who is the thinker, without Dave Bob would surely be doing a five-thousand-year stretch. Bob often repays this loyalty with threats and promises to punch his fucking head in, even through all of this they're inseparable, Bob without Dave is like fish without chips, or the desert without sand, together with a fist like Thanos they command the streets, where everyone is fair game, and the streets are the Serengeti, dealers are like zebra or deer, and Bob is the lion with Teesside being his pride rock. You see we come from good stock. Dave is one of eight, all men, and he learned his trade well from the best you could say, his elders all having their own crew and different trades, from shoplifting on mass to car stereos, fraud, sheds and counterfeit goods, fake notes and cheque books, his world was a cave of struggles and victories, he learned it all by simply watching, and asking the odd question.

His friends were the kind of friends you need in any situation with even the big men of Teesside, Dave is the one that is unseen, but the one you know is there, legend has it that you feel his presence like a ghostly shiver n tha or that draught that tickles your spine when the window is left open, long before Bob comes blundering through the door, you see Dave wants to be in the room without being noticed, he wants to be that man on the inside, but bob wants the world to know he's arrived, taking doors off their hinges and throwing hand grenades is more like Bob's style, Dave wanted to be in the room and attack from within. He is the logistical master that you never question, you would never know where the shooter came from, or where it was going after it was used, you never needed to ask. Bob would ask for something and Dave just made it happen.

Now don't get me wrong, Dave could Fry his own bacon, he just did it slightly differently, but no matter how we worked this place everything was 50/50. To this very day folks can never quite understand how this combination of personalities worked, we just know it did.It's like Bob is on a seemingly short chain ready to pounce and his pal holds it, tort, this isn't to say Bob won't turn and bite because we know this happens regularly.

Since the early days, Dave was the ignored voice of reason, he was always frustrated because he knew there were other ways to achieve the same outcome. So where does this all begin? How did the unhinged little bastard himself become such a lion amongst the hyenas? This Dave, how does he survive walking with such a caged animal on the loose, Let me take you on a journey into the mind of a madman, through the eyes and mind as close up as it gets, I am Dave.

"SOUND AS FUCK ARNA."

BOB

The Early Days...

So, where it all starts, should we go back to the birth of this fucking monster? Sadly it is where it all began, 1970 June I believe, somewhere in the heart of the steelworks and Furness', the sky's alight with the devil's flames, in the burn off that can only be described as hell on Earth. A toddler was born, his mother was in labour only seconds Bob did not want to fuck about a moment longer sliding out windmilling, he knew at this stage there was money to be made and no shit bag was getting in his way. Bob came out of his own free will, when he was ready, he needed no one, he came with a built-in fixed frown and no reason to smile, fists clenched tight in a boxer's stance and his mother insisting that he wore a tiny version of the Teesside belcher.Whilst looking around the room like he had been here before, Bob knew that he had to get out of this place if he was to survive, the sound of other shit bags screaming and looking for attention was not his bag.

And so the helpless little monster with a tiny little attitude had to play ball, he knew he had to go along with what all these big people wanted, but he was to bide his time remembering all their faces, taking snapshots with his photographic built-in memory camera, because one day he will be punching all their fucking heads in. That cute little frown was staying put, it was going nowhere, and some say that his first word uttered was not Mama or Dada, it was in actual fact "eh".

Bob was born 5lb 3oz he knew he was vulnerable, he needed carbs and fast, he would look around at all the other little bastards on the ward realising that he needed to grow. He knew that all these other screaming little rats could possibly be his competition in life, these were the mutants that were to pay their way in this town. There is an old tale once told by a grown man that his earliest memories were that of himself laid in a crib on a hospital ward, and another baby grabbing him by the throat and taking his food, muttering some shite like "blurh blah blurh blah fucking head in" was this Bob? Who knows, it has all the hallmarks of the first ever tax, maybe this was where the thirst for it came from I guess we will never know.

Then there is Dave (me) and my arrival was much slicker. I was here 9 months earlier, I took my time, no fuss, all back of the bus, I needed to blend in with every other little toe rag, I was sent early to make plans, a bit like the movie terminator. I knew there was a reason so I began to pave the way set things up as it were, and so I played ball and never really got involved with the politics of the ward. I would rarely cry, and when alone with the other little new-born mutants I would ask about Bob, "any of you cunts seen the big man?" There is a rumour, that at 2 days old I whispered to the midwife "has Bob arrived"? But this has never been verified, and she phoned in sick the next day, let's just say that the midwife was never seen again after this.

I worked very differently I would give food to the other new-borns to gain their trust, you never know when you need information, this was Teesside's new-born spillers, and I wanted them to remember me. Even in the early newborn days, it was easy to see just how this relationship was about to develop, me the thinker, the sound rational mind and my bolshie friend who didn't understand what fucks were, never mind giving them out!We were a match and nobody even knew it, my job was to make sure my big person made contact with Bob's adult carer, fuck knows how but it was to happen. Like cyborgs from the future, us two cunts were destined to meet, brains and brawn in a match that was to rock the backward town of Teesside.

*"DON'T INTERRUPT ME AGAIN WHILST I'M TALKING!
I'LL SNAP YA JAW YA DAFT CUNT."*

Bob

2

Growing up was Tough

Growing up was tough, it was all about survival and who you can trust, Bob trusted no one not even the woman that cuddled him morning noon and night, she had an agenda that Bob kept an eye on, what was the old bag after? What did she want? The same woman that gave him his protein in a bottle ten times a day and spoke shit he couldn't understand would pass him around other big people like he was spliff loaded with green an all tha, this little bastard was getting fed up of this baby malarkey and would make for the door as soon as he could crawl, with every intention of making it on his own.They soon realised, that little prison bars were needed for the doorways to keep the bastard in. He knew out there, beyond the two hundred foot prison fence that was specially designed to keep him in, there was serious money to be made, and it didn't matter who or how. Bob would rattle the bars like a little ape caged yards from the jungle, frustrated, angry, and nobody was listening.

At this stage in my toddlership I was walking and learning to talk this shit myself, looking for a way out, we always looked for a way out, you see we could make it on our own we believed that. I would be checking the raw steel bars in the doorway for weak spots, accidentally turning off the monitor to time the quick responses of the big people, still shitting in little pads and having grownups clean it up pure protein, like that smell in the gym from the big lad benching three ton, who you know only eats eggs ten million at a time, the guy who Me and Bob have yet to meet, but I know he's out there. There is a story that is within the family that my first word was "Bob", not Mam or Dad, fuck knows.

Our paths crossed one summer's day, I pointed to the sand as we drove along the seafront, making some crazy noise that actually translated to "stop the fucking car" my mother catching on and pulling over for a stroll along Redcar beach, I was on foot because by now I was planning my way out of this shit hole, all I needed to do was get rid of these reins and I was free. In the distance I could see another little one being pushed in some sort of device with wheels, it was Bob. I didn't know this at the time, but we were heading for them, all I could see was a toddler giving his mother a hard time. We headed towards them like two cars in a head on collision with no breaks and the drivers are both asleep at the wheel, the impact was an explosion that rocked ICI, it was Bob and Dave meeting for the first time.

Teesside was about to change forever. When I think back I often would catch this little bastard staring out over the North Sea, pointing at the tiny little unrecognisable four-legged beast that occasionally would breath fire, over the horizon, with flying machines landing and taking off every moment, he would hold his arms out, fingers clutching open and closed, frantic and he would lunge forward like it was his home, I never quite understood why, or what that was about. As our grownups passed each other and spoke their language I made eye contact with Bob and gave him a little nod muttering the words "awwright", he frowned and gave me a look, and said "I'm alright you alright eh you what", I replied back instantly with "well sound then". It was then that I knew, this was the cunt I was looking for. "Bob" I smiled crouched down to his level to introduce myself properly, and I immediately noticed the frown, before I knew what was happening the little bastard slapped me with one hand and took my milk lolly with the other, not a flinch just that stare, "well go on then, fuck off" he mumbled. In that moment I accepted my fate in the same way as I accept it in the grown up world, nothing changed from that very moment, I always remember that was the first time Bob punched my fucking head in, I rubbed my cheek and gazed at this little gobshite and had an overwhelming sense of protection towards him, I knew he needed protein and to start lifting as soon as possible, the tiny little shitbag arms needed size. Our grownups become close friends which was perfect for Bob and me, we got on with the job in hand, and that was to make money, Teesside was about to become ours, as early as next week, I found my partner, and he found me, we just needed to find a decent gym and some lowlifes to play with.

Sooner or later Bob learned how to walk, now this might seem cute, but there was nothing he ever did that could be described as cute, this is when things would become interesting, there was a couple of mutants in the street, the same age give or take ten minutes, Bod and Fabio, these two little bastards had all the best gear little push scooters, battery powered Range Rover and guns. Bob had a thing or two for guns, a passion that never really left us.If there was ever a moment when Bob began his career it was now, Bob wanted that range rover and to get it he knew things would have to get real, in true to lifestyle I would be the brains behind pulling this fucker off, Bob just had to trust me and be patient.

Over the next few days, I would watch them in the garden and engage in chatting baby shit in order to gain their trust, just when things were going in our favour, these little fuckers were about to hand over the keys with a smile, and a blessing, in stomps Bob with his bumbling unsteady strut, looking like he just beat the local deadlift record before I could babble at him to stop the shitbag from next door was dragged out of the driver's seat, as easy as that, "eh you what" screams Bob standing over him like a heavyweight champ seconds away from the victory, and before he could scream, Bob wheel spun off at a top speed of 2.1 MPH! I remember slapping my hand off my forehead and thinking, fuck sake, before jumping into the passenger seat with not a clue where we were going.Truth is we were only ever going to get as far as the garden gate. This was Bob's first rap, it felt good to take what was not ours, but in his head, that Range Rover was always Bob's, from the moment it was bought for the two little rats, even if it was only for 4 mins, till Bob's mother smashed him up and returned the keys, with a grown-up apology. We weren't sorry one bit and Bob never forgets a face, that little cunt cost Bob a Range Rover and that was going to come back and bite him on the arse.

As the coming months passed we found ourselves doing hard time behind the bars of the baby gate for snatching some sweets off a bunch of kids, that would have given us them if only for the asking.It wasn't about the sweets it was about keeping these cunts in line before we knew it the little people in Bob's nursery were handing over the k-ly like it was grown up nose candy. We had that place boxed off, arriving late,distribution and collection of goods, with the occasional table of Lego getting flipped in anger as a distraction, while I mooch around in the kid's lunch boxes for extra protein, it was all about protein.

We had a system and it worked Bob would go ape and smash up the joint shouting at the teacher "al punch your fucking head in" and I would be like James Bond sliding around unseen collecting the loot, we needed to grow and fast and this was our only way. This place was full of little shit bags who were growing at the same pace potentially becoming our rivals it was important to be ahead of the game.

By now communication was improving and we could string sentences together, even if it was only things like "you what?", "ere you" and "well aye", this was enough to get by and get us what we needed.

The grown-up people in our lives had no idea that Bob and Dave were moving forward at a rate they couldn't keep up with. In our empty heads, we were getting older than them, they knew fuck all. Primary school was not an easy patch to own, there were mutants that had grown up shit bags looking after them, with high and tight shaved heads and half of a uniform, and mini Nike trainers just like Dads, usually arriving at school on a quad bike along the footpath with not a fuck to give, with Dad wearing his big gold belcher chain, oversized bracelet and dirty tracksuit.We knew that these were the cockroaches we needed to keep in tow if we were to survive in this yard, we knew that every kid in here was afraid of these lowlifes, accept us, these germs were ours, all we needed was the right fucking bleach. So this was Bob and Dave's daytime prison, shanking these maggots with a lollipop stick in assembly fast and hard wasn't that uncommon.

Survival was not easy but Bob had an advantage, he had back up we were a team, and if these little parasites thought we were cheating at marbles we probably were, so fuck, what about it ya daft cunts, Bob will punch fuck out of every single one of them. If needs be I would let Bob swing his tiny little arms like Viv Graham in a nightclub doorway, for me, this was always a last resort, for Bob it was the first port of call.

Playtime was always like holding a position against ISIS, that part of the tarmac in the playground that always had a mysterious and unknown power, was always our patch and we fought many a gang of scumbags to hold it.Me n Bob back to back with no ammunition other than our puny little arms, this is where that stolen extra protein was to come in handy.

The shitbags have a plan, ten to one, their idea was to attack our land in numbers, pick us off one at a time twenty fists on to four, then retell the story around the classroom how it was one on one, and how little Bodsa and Bob were "toe to toe", this bloating of the truth was something that kind of stayed with Teesside.Strangely, nowadays the tough guy always wins, well in the story, and if you can actually get them to perform the stories they become the mortar of social club shit talk.

After the onslaught there were only two people who knew the truth, then the bell would ring and it was back to the bullshit that primary school was really all about. After any conflict was over, the respect restored, partly because these maggots were alone, not in their numbers and more vulnerable than a teenager in Rotherham.Thinking back nothing much has changed here, it is still the same Teesside, it stands firm and with it so do its morals.

So, this was primary school it consisted of guarding a piece of playground land, mooching lunchboxes for protein and keeping shit bags in line, we never forgot that these little losers were our competitors in whatever it was we thought we were going to do when we got big, and this always gave us the edge, this lot were being kids and growing up, we just wanted to do the growing bit, we were far too serious to have a childhood.

We were focused on the prize, we didn't have time for Miss Gibbons the teacher, even though she flirted with Bob like a Boro lass running out of bugle on a Saturday night, she didn't stand a chance, Bob was not interested in the smash.

So the playground tussles paid off, our patch of tarmac was untouched, we sold Mojo's and Black Jacks all day, well we never, we had that boxed off.Primary school was starting to look like the Cadre building from "New Jack City" everything running smoothly, cash in, goods out, we were like pimps, with plenty of enemies, trying to cut a side deal like G money, these bitches wanted a piece of the action but had no idea how to get it.

The Betrayal...

Betrayal was rife, these little rats would pass on information about their next attack for a sherbet dib dab, and half a tip top.You see nothing has really changed since the early days, being passed a betting slip in the bogs with "half ten Smigga" written on it was not that uncommon, the exchange would take place like soviet spies in a packed café, we were masters at this and these little rodents loved a Wham bar.

Now,Smigga was the school's dysfunctional kid, the one that had social services on speed dial and child protection on a stakeout. He was the one who had one Mother and a handful of Dads, depending on the day of the week, the one who regularly spent time outside the headmaster's office for something he did not do, yea ok if you believe that shit, he was the one with the risky haircut that looked like a dead rat slapped on his head that his Thursday MMADad gave him, the one that could penny for the guy over Aldi whilst his Mother was at the bingo. I often wondered where the disloyal selfish maggots that still run through the town ever came from, and now I know. So after the exchange of information watching them scurry off back to the opposite end of the yard to re-join their leaders, with fake smiles and pockets full of well-earned candy that was being distributed to everybody like poison, was kind of satisfying, watching them eat the goods, that surely can only taste of utter betrayal and that had paid for their demise.

This was the easy bit, the difficult part was working out if this was all a big set up and Bob just handed over our candy for a double bluff. Bob hated nothing more than to be betrayed by the rats that are betraying themselves.

I often thought that Bob had distinct early psychopathic tendencies, and I was his personal psychiatrist, I kept a lid on this little unhinged bastard, I was the voice that said to him "breathe", it didn't always work still doesn't even today. For a moment I would pause waiting for the next move, while Bob was like the mastiff in the yard, repeating over and over "al punch his fucking head in", stretching the chain he can't break, wanting to windmill the lot of them all by himself. The other side never really wanted to challenge us but I was curious about the betting slip and the time of ten thirty written in shitbag handwriting, I looked over at their squad, no Smigga, where was this little termite, was he being re-homed like a new puppy by a social worker? Or was he hiding? I counted heads and got confused, these bastards all look the same, same haircuts, same striped jumpers, and all doing the imaginary pad work with the weaker member.Still no Smigga, I look down at my watch 10:27, Bob looks like he has rabies determined to snap that ten inch collar, still no Smigga, I stare at the betting slip hoping the time has changed but it still says half ten Smigga what did this mean? I look at my watch again 10:29 shit is getting real, there is a moment of pause, things slow down almost to a standstill, these shitbags are looking over like they know something we don't, but no Smigga. Bob stands still one final check of the time and you could hear the second hand click into place the whole yard heard it, then an almighty whack from the side sounded like a pure charge sheet on a Saturday night. The Boro ghost shot, Bob falls to his knees and Smigga is off before he realises the trouble he has landed himself in. All I can do is smile over at these vermin and nod, there is a silent appreciation for what just happened, an unspoken congratulations for this was a very temporary victory and it was a bit like Leicester winning the premier league. The cunt just ghosted my pal, and so now it all made sense the ghost shot coincided with the bell going for the end of break, which meant no retaliation a mean these little bastards were all about the ghost shot, Teesside is all about the ghost shot. Now they have the time to adjust the event amongst the hangers on. Story has it that Smigga walked over to Bob and they were toe to toe for an hour, eventually, Bob gave up and Smigga was victorious, a mean that is how it usually goes in this place, that's how Teesside operates, and then when the listeners add their bit to it, and their listeners add their bit, well Bob is usuallyin ICU and Smigga is now the kiddie, you get my drift, you see there will never be any actual rumble, just the talk of it and a one sided version of events is all people need, you see the pattern?

What usually follows such a betrayal is amnesia, these mongrels forget half of everything that they do, and when the bullshit version of Smigga's victory dies down, it's like it never happened, but it did happen didn't it?! Oh yes, it did and Bob and Dave have been thinking about this moment since before Bob took a knee after the ghost shot that day.

The ghost shot is legendary around Teesside, for the perpetrator it is well planned, well thought out, the timing is better than Greenwich, the shitbag will execute it with precision, it usually happens at the bar, or in a takeaway shop, if you're unlucky enough you could be with the wife doing absolutely nothing.The ghost shot does not discriminate, nor does it need a reason it doesn't have rules or boundaries, the ghost shot may be a repayment for making eye contact nine years ago with the coward that throws it, it may even be that the ghost is delivered because "you bucked our lass" twenty years ago before they were born, hard to fathom I know.

Once the ghost has been delivered the perpetrator has an uncanny ability to re-enact the whole event In a somewhat more creative and unbelievable Bruce Lee style. It has always been a mystery to me where this evil act ever came from, and why people do it but I guess on reflection back to our younger days, Smigga answers that one and thinking about it Smigga, he has his own grown up, who is also a shitbag, this place has a tendency to breed likeminded fledglings, offspring that mirror grown up behaviour and it is not uncommon for this behaviour to be forced upon the little innocent blank canvas, yes the ghost is Teesside's very own, sadly we are claiming this manoeuvre and anyone who tries to copy it, watch out for the betting slip.

Bob goes all 'Viv'...

Back to it, Bob is head hunting he wants blood, he's still muttering "al punch that cunt out" whereas me I am looking at this from a different angle, I want Smigga and the little bastards who exchanged the betting slip for our goods to worry a little. In real grown up worlds, these kids are nothing on their own,I am starting to see a real similarity to today's folk. After the lunch bell goes and we are being warned about playing aggressive games in the yard we have only one thing on our minds. The dust has settled the stories are simply old fish and chip newspaper, the rats have forgotten all the details of what happened, things are back to normal Smigga and his band of jumble sale wearing vagrants that play one sided football in the corner, and the girls on the other side who believe Smigga and his boys are the ones to be seen with, getting excited when there is a goal in off the jumper, and flirting with skipping ropes and touie balls off the wall singing shit songs that make no sense about sailing across the water, the teacher and his cup of coffee strutting about like a periscope watching, seeing all like a giant referee. Amongst all the normality there is me n Bob, all I can hear him saying is "am goanna punch his fucking head in" this phrase was to become the DNA of Bob, it was a phrase that was to become the first words out of his mouth in any situation.

So, in true little people gangland fashion we strolled over to their patch just me and Bob so the world could see, hands out of our pockets palms showing side by side, at this point the rats do what rats do when they're afraid, and scurry about with no direction. We approach the doorway, which was their land, we are confronted with one of the more daring of the mob, in the corner there was a small CCTV camera that was covered in cobwebs, but Bob did not give a shit, almost like he knew it was there and wanted it to record the whole thing. By now we are well and truly in personal space, people are uncomfortable, the schoolyard is watching, Bob slipped Mr white the periscope a couple of jumbo flumps as payment to drink his coffee over the other side of the yard, "ere there's two flumps ya daft cunt now fuck off we have business to sort" I mean we have these shitbags right where we want them.

Bob stares into Smiggas soul and says "ere a wanna word" the girl he was stood with wants to leave, I tell her to stay where she is, she needs to see this. Bob like a hurricane begins his assault throwing left then right his puny little seven year old arms each one landing like an airplane on the runway, " go on Bob, go on Bob" I am shouting, "that's it Bob, go on Bob", I don't need to intervene I just look at the rats, that says it all, they can move in and clean up when we are done.The teacher is earning his flumps and blind eyeing the whole thing, "shouldn't you be somewhere fucking else" I shout to Mr White, and thousand yard stare the cunt, as the so called tough kid falls to the ground and I am now pulling the dog off him, this story cannot be told in a

27

different way, no one can add a little seasoning, Smigga was a shitbag and we just took his doorway with ease, we didn't want to own this door, no what we wanted was to show the yard that we could have it if we wanted.

All in a day's work and the home time bell has not even gone, Mr White gave us the nod and the look that said "pleasure doing business boys" the rats scrape up off the floor what was left of little Smigga and we strolled across the playground like a victorious Prince Naseem.

Home time was always a great moment but always left us a little vulnerable, I would look for my big person and Bob would search for his, there were times when we would be alone, separated, I would describe this as when you have a rough night on the doors and are painted in someone else's claret, but have to walk back to your own car at three in the morning, it is a scary moment you need eyes 360 degrees. Finding our adults at three thirty after the bell goes, was like the moment you pull away in your car, a sense of complete relief that cliché "another day another dollar" racing through your mind in rhythm with the heart pounding like that drum and bass track you love. In the arms of your adult making eye contact with your wing man, and giving a nod was the best feeling ever, we made it and it was all to repeat the very next day. For Smigga, who climbed on the back of his stolen quad bike, with his 'spliff behind the ear' dysfunctional stepdad, the story was showing off his wounds of the day adding his touch of artistic license, and getting the "well done kidda" backwards praise, this was enough to keep this little termite in the game.

For us, it was sketty on toast, and hoping that our adults popped in for coffee so we could re-group count our loot and make plans for the next shift.We relied on our big people a mean, they were the ones who gave us lifts and sorted out the grub.

By now the protein was kicking in and I would often see Bob doing a really shit double bicep pose, or most muscular that he had seen on television, by some fake wrestler in the states, he would look in the mirror that leaned against his

28

mother's bedroom wall amongst the scattered cheap makeup, and borrowed stilettos. There was one time I walked in and Bob was looking right at himself in the same mirror, left foot forward, knees slightly bent, chin firmly on his chest shoulder forward staring, with the frown that has been carved into his face with a chisel and had been there seven years, fists clenched as he utters them now infamous words "eh al punch your fucking head in", at this very moment I let out a sigh, I couldn't help but conclude that this was a little bastard I was dealing with, a pure cunt, I remember shaking my head and I knew that this little protein filled nasty trouble maker was going to give me a lifetime headache, I knew that as his psychiatrist I would have to put together a treatment plan that would keep us both safe in this shit hole we call Teesside.

"I GREW UP IN BERWICK HILLS AND I BELIEVED IN SANTA CLAUS UNTIL I WAS 9, BUT I'D HEARD OF BOB & DAVE WHEN I WAS 8".

JAMIE BOYLE AUTHOR/FILMMAKER

The Heist...

I never worried about the future, I was only eight, but I could see how things were going to turn out.One night after school I made my way up to Bobs den in his bedroom, the den was serious stuff, so listen up. I had to use the correct password to gain entry, this joint was not for any mug, it was constructed of quilts and cushions, it was usually dark with a shit torch in the corner and had some sort of painful consequence should you get the password wrong.I learned the hard way and had the password wrote on my arm in pen, after successful entry I was about to witness a jaw dropping moment, Bob was in the den with a big persons hack saw that he had stolen from the toolbox, and his tin pan alley rifle was getting a facelift, he had already taken the butt off, and was halfway through sawing the barrel, yes I know what you're thinking, or maybe I don't or maybe I don't want to know. "What the fuck are you doing?" I whispered, "you're gonna get us nicked." Bob always replied with "eh" which was closely followed with "shut ya fucking mouth", it's an old gun I've had it ten years" a mean there was no need to do the maths we were eight years old for fuck sake. Shaking my head and wondering where this was going I cautiously asked, "what's happening?" "You will see, you will see" was his reply. I was now in my 'thinking about the consequences' mode, I was doing what I do best, thinking of how I could get us both out of whatever was about to happen. I usually do this very well and always have a plan but this time Bob had something on his mind and I wasn't about to get in his way, I just knew I had to be in this shoulder to shoulder. The plan was me and Bob were about to rob the bedroom bank, a jar of money that had been there since we started our sweet racket in school. The shooter was ready, Bob put on his favourite Scooby doo hoodie, hood up he pulled the cord tight looking at himself in the mirror holding his new baby, what a devastatingly disturbing little bastard he was becoming, god knows what was going through his eight year old underdeveloped mind, all I could do was pray this was all going to work.

Bob shouts his sister upstairs who is only five and as gullible as a Boro coke rat that believes his last bag of dropped off dust was "pure". In she strolls carrying her rag doll which was later to be used as a hostage in what was about to become our very own dog day afternoon. It was this poor little mite that Bob was to use in the hold up, she was a cashier, "quick get in here" Bob shouted.A mean she thought it was exciting and just did as she was told, looking pretty behind the makeshift counter with loot that already belonged to us. I was still trying to figure out how we could explain all of this to our grownups.Bob just wanted the loot and to create the drama that was about to unfold.

Now, there are many ways to rob a post office we needed to be in and out fast no one hurt, I timed the adults coming upstairs I knew we had 45 seconds door to floor, we needed to be in and out in less than 30. I went over this ten times with Bob, "no one gets hurt ok Bob" I had to tell him in a commanding voice, I then got threatened with "who are you talking to ya daft cunt?" followed by him sticking the shotgun under my chin, "relax Bob easy does it mate it's me, take your finger off the trigger, that's it breathe, easy does it mate, back to business."

Bob had stolen a cardboard box earlier that day and stashed it out the way that was the getaway car, the engine was the noise he made from his mouth along with the sound of the screeching breaks, as we pulled up outside the bedroom I distinctly remember saying in and out fast and quiet, this was going to be anything but, Bob wanted the full shootout you aren't taking me alive malarkey, if Bob was going then so was I. Hood up,Bob kicked open his door, standing there was his cute little sister with pigtails and a ragdoll looking like she was selling stamps and postal orders, she smiled at us like we were all pals, clueless, whilst babysitting a copper jar that was soon to be ours.Pointing his shooter to the ceiling, he let off a shot, cocked his weapon, and another, then one more he shouts, "get on the fucking floor" he shoves the shooter straight into his sisters face and she looks at him like he's a stranger, I can almost read her tiny mind saying "who the fuck is this idiot?", Bob snatches the ragdoll and thrusts the gat into its mush, now he has his sisters attention, she drops to the floor and begs for the life of her doll, I am by the door with the stopwatch, fifteen seconds in Bob wants the vault, "there is no fucking vault" I shouted whilst grabbing the jar and Bob is still in his element, it's like he was waiting for the law to turn up so he can have his moment, me, on the other hand, am not about that life but Bob is my pal, and that's all there is to it. Bob turns to an imaginary security guard who looks like he wants to be a hero standing there like Clint Eastwood had just flicked his poncho over his shoulder, Bob screams "keep your fucking hands where I can see them" this is like a western draw, tumbleweed passing, church bell making a louder noise than ever. Bob pointing his shooter from the hip, the imaginary guard has to draw from the holster, thirty seconds in, a bead of sweat from Bob's brow hits the floor with a splash, we are breaking the rules in and out, but this guard wants to make the front page he wants Bob, the make believe man in uniform flinches, boom Bob lets him have it, at the same time I shout "noooooooo" the invisible guard drops to floor backwards, in slow motion. "Bob let's get the fuck out of here" I tug on his puny little arm he turns eyes bulging, I thought I was next, "did you get the money?" Bob shouts, "course I fucking did, now let's move." Bob insisted we take the ragdoll for insurance, I wanted to let the scruffy little bastard go, but Bob always gets his own way.

Using his voice he screeched away from the bedroom to the sounds of the old bill nee nor nee nor, "fucking step on it" he yelled it's the filth, "take your next left, now right, step on it" shouts Bob in my ear!In my calm tone,I needed to take control of this situation, I was the driver "just relax and sit back I think we have lost them." I had no idea what we had gotten ourselves into but this was next level. In the distance we could hear shouting "Bob Dave, your tea's are ready bring your sister down" "ok mum we're coming" was the only reply we could give we were starving it had been a long night, Bob muttering to himself "this cunt better have me a Parmo" when really tinned ravioli and burnt French fries was about our whack. Off we went downstairs for our grub, little sister snatching her ragdoll out of the motor and not really understanding what just happened but giving us the evils, narrow eyeing her stupid brother all the way past us. Bob had stolen his money but it was never about the money, ever. Everywhere we went Bob always left me thinking either, what the fuck just happened there or what the fuck are we about to do, this was a combination of the two. I had to regroup my thoughts and think of a plan to get out of any mess he left behind. I just knew life was either gonna be easy or very difficult with this bastard.

"I HAVE BUILT MY EMPIRE UPON FEAR AVANA."

BOB

3

The Standoff

Playing outside in the open was where Bob was most at home, jumping off shed roofs onto piss stained mattresses at heights Hollywood would question was the norm, or playing army's with bits of wood when the sole aim was to murder your pal from down the street.Bob was always chucking hand grenades about then punching some cunts head in for not dying in the most animated way possible. There was a council board den that we built as some sort of clubhouse where we would sesh on pop and crisps it was built in the back garden with a doorway drizzled in nannas old curtains.Some serious shit went down in these places, loud music and claret decorated the place.

I always remember Bob allowing the local shitbags in, which was odd because nobody got in for no reason, there was a plan manifesting that I knew nothing about but I knew I had to back it. After Bob consumed the sweets and pop these maggots brought it was time for them to leave, "come on lads time to go" Bob commanded, "howay Bob we brought sweets" whispered one of the locals quite daringly to be fair. I looked at Bob he looked at me we said nothing which was a language in its self, "a don't give a fuck" saidBob who is now in the stance and my ears suddenly pricked up. I have my eyes on everyone, no cunt is ghosting my pal here not again, Bob, Craggy, Bongo, and some other lowlife, are up on their feet, "al snap your jaw you daft little cunt!"Bob is focused on the mouth that dared speak, this is it, it's going off everyone is now in the stance, empty pop bottles everywhere, the whole den is game as fuck, the place stinks of proper Boro, the smell of sneaky sly 'we will only take you in our numbers bastard' filled the air. Bob and me are about to redecorate the place with a new shade of

Teesside shitbag, see I am already on top of the safest way to deal with this saloon standoff, "finish your drink and fuckoff" Bob points to the curtain, we are both now left foot forward, chins tucked in, and then in a calm scared tone Bongo the quiet one mumbles with absolute confidence "you put us out." "Eh you wha? Al punch your fucking head in" Bob screams. This is where I step in, I usually have to step in at this point because someone is going to get hurt. "Lads do us a favour, we've had a good night let's not spoil it, come back again next week." With one hand on Bob's chest and the other helping these idiots towards the door, things start moving fast,Bob's breathing is filling the den, "eh" Bob yells, he can't believe there is someone cheeky enough to stand-off like this, the only thing stopping carnage right now is me, and I can't hold this fort much longer. I now have four sets of eyes trained on fists, Bob is like a scrapyard pooch Cujo that lives in that old ford Cortina and covered in oil.The three shitbags are thinking just like Teessider's, they want to take Bob in numbers, it's how it works sadly. I try one more time, "look lads leave it, do yourselves a favour and just go," still nothing,it's been like this for what feels like two hours, staring, the only thing moving is our eyes. I look at Bob in my peripheral and he's doing the same, I nod, he nods, then I drop my arm to my side, you see that is the only thing that was stopping Bob from doing his thing, it was like I gave him permission, he grabs onto the leader and rains a barrage of shots, he hits the floor, the other two aren't sure so I make eye contact, "I don't think so" I said in a tone that was designed to help them out with friendly advice. Bob is finishing the job and these two, by now, can see that it's not worth it, this cunt screams like a girl, in a rear choke full of claret Bob drags the socalled leader to the door and ejects him, through Nana's curtain and onto the charcoal patch that was once a bommie, with the contempt he deserved, he rolls down the garden and whips out a toy mobile phone and flips it open like fucking Captain Kirk calling the big brother he doesn't have.

Now, there is just one on one, these two know the deal, they understand that they can't shout threats of revenge or retaliation until they get into the garden and are backing off, so it's a peaceful exit hands in the air like this was a stick up, all palms are showing this was tense, I slap one of them across the mouth to install some humiliation. Bob wanted to go ahead again, "keep moving lads" I ushered these maggots closer to the way out, we all move to the door silently and all three mutants are now out of the den, then in true Teesside fashion, the predictable verbal onslaught begins.

"Come on then, me and you round here," shouts one of the creatures, who was surprisingly quiet a moment ago, "howay me and you ya fat bastard" he homes in on Bob, keeping a distance of about three miles, "you won't fight me will ya?Ya fucking shithouse, me and you one on one." That's all we can hear, but our work was done here we knew this, and so did the injured one who stared at Bob throughout the whole ordeal, and was the one who brought this to a close, "come on let's go power rangers is on soon," moaned the injured rat as he limps away, now we know where the stance came from.

Occasionally, me and Bob would look at each other and laugh, Icouldn't help but feel that sense of dread and worry that Bob was making enemies fast, that meant if Bob had enemies, then so did I, the difference being that I gave a fuck, and Bob didn't. I can never get that image out of my head, Bob standing there on the door, curtain blowing, it was sturdy, made from stolen council boards, with his little proteinfilled skinny arms folded, it was an image that was to become too familiar. Bob looked comfortable and happy standing there pleased with what had just happened, it was after the event that I would ask "what the fuck was that?" I never asked this during any incident, my job was to back this nutcase up and deal with the fallout later, "I never liked them three shitbags anyway shut ya fucking mouth". Bob laughed went back into the den to salvage any sweets that we earned, me, I would just be left standing thinking about the next time we would meet these little rats, and how we would maintain the respect especially in the playground.

The Rivals...

The best nights were sleepovers, our adults would meet up and I would usually bail mine at the end of the coffee, it might look something like this, "come on Dave let's get you home, school tomorrow" Mother would say. My reply was quick and simple, Ididn't give a fuck, "you get off home I'm fucking staying right here, me and Bob got shit to sort out." Well to be honest that was the fantasy version, it would be more like, "be good for aunty Ann." We would smile and nod that sort of thing.Mother was a force to reckon with, we all got along nicely, then we knew we were in for a long night, straight upstairs to the den, passwords needed obviously.

The two new kids across the street needed discussing, Bob did not like the look of these two cunts, but then what did Bob ever really like? I am trying the, let's see how we go approach, I want to see if we can use them in some way, form an alliance maybe, after all, they might be good lads. Bob had other plans, he wanted to railroad into their souls, smash them up and tell them it was our fucking street and set up a direct debit payment plan for fucking breathing

If they wanted to live here there were rules, pecking orders, and understandings to be made clear. "Whoa fuck sake Bob, let's give these kids a break, we know fuck all about them and they may be ok," I said nervously holding my arms out in front of me, to stop both of his arms should they feel the need to punch my fucking head in, he was already raging at the thought of cutting these two strangers some slack. But, for the first time, I was winning, Bob was willing to give them five minutes. "Well sound then, but a swear down if they're shit al punch their fucking heads in" raged Bob, "awrightawright" I mumbled, it now felt like I was doing these maggots a favour, and we don't do favours unless there is a fee attached.

So, we waited until the next day to make our presence known, we sat in next doors range rover that was left out all night in the rain, arms out the window, staring over the road, "take it easy Bob, let's just see what happens" I murmured, trying to sound like I was in control of this situation. Bob is at the wheel, his eyes locked onto the biggest of the pair, who really hadn't even realised we were there, these two fuckers were just kicking the ball in the garden, then Bob lets the frown out of the bag. "Look at these daft cunts, they think they're fucking rock hard, kicking the ball like they can play footy, I am not having it" warned Bob, "hang on mate they're only kicking the ball," I said shaking my head, this was going in one direction in spite of what we agreed last night in the club. These two stopped playing footy, and glared over locking onto Bob, "eh al punch.." Iinterrupted him rudely, "I know mate I will too."We started up the motor and pulled off the drive looking like miniature shit versions of Pat Tate & Tony Tucker as we drove past at 2.2 MPH, we slowed down to 1.8, we wanted these bastards to know it was them we were interested in, all eyes locked on and Bob cannot contain himself any longer, "eh, awright?" Bob shouts, he stops the motor and loosens the belt, what felt like an hour was only a few seconds, then comes the response from their garden "I'm alright you awright?" said this big kid who Bob had taken an instant dislike to before we were even in the motor. Bob leaped out of the range rover and was in the stance, which meant I was to follow you know how this works. This was becoming all too familiar so I had to change tactics, the riot police were probably already on the way, I needed to slow things down before the whole street got smashed up. I decided to introduce myself, giving the nod, I confidently said, "now then, I'm Dave, and this is Bob, what's the crack?" Bob who is still in the stance, he is still trained on the big lad, there was going to be no ghosting round here, "Now then lads, I'm jones, and this is my pal Khanage" replied the big fella, I looked at Bob and he really wanted to check out why this little bastard called himself Khanage, part of me wanted the same, but remember this was my call not Bobs. After this interaction I backed off slowly to the motor, tapping Bob on the chest and whispering, "let's go mate, another time, there are too many witnesses."Under his breath, Bob's whispering "fucking Khanage, Khanage, al punch his fucking head in." Biting my teeth together flexing my jaw muscles and thinking yea, we will see you around, we needed these two to realise who we were, and what we were about, "see you around yea" I shouted, "well aye" Khanage mumbled. Into the car and our blacked-out windows rolled up, I couldn't let them see Bob raging in the front passenger seat, "I'm having them two" insisted Bob, "I know bro, I know". Bob was fuming, yelling in the car "I want a one on one with Khanage Dave sort it out".

Off we went top speed and we got the feeling that nothing was really achieved by the whole situation other than these two cunts had met Bob and Dave for the first time. I could not help but think these two might be good lads, we might be able to use them, Bob and I were making a lot of enemies fast, we needed to slow the battlefield down and gather some soldiers. This was very much my way of thinking and Bob just wanted to crush everything, his little brain was full of ideas an adult couldn't process.

As the winter months closed in on us we would see less of each other partly due to the shit weather and our grownups not leaving the house, fire on bored shitless we had a town to run and that's all that mattered. Over the next few years things did not really change, we gathered enemies like they were football cards, it didn't really bother us, but we collected some soldiers too, remember the two shitbags across the road? Yea Jones and Khanage, well Bob had his one on one in his garden and we put that to bed, he made a mess of Khanage now we have an unspoken respect for each other, we just nod and maybe say "awright?"No need to talk about it, it's just there.

We outgrew the range rover that next door used to leave outside in the rain so we sold that to some dick head off another estate. Me and Bob were always still back to back, we'd outgrown the den out the back and regularly scuffled with the shit bags off other estates.Smigga would occasionally make an appearance over the park with a handful of rats on stolen scooters only stopping to make ten seconds of eye contact with Bob like that good hiding wasn't finished.

Somehow, our world was very unsettled the enemies had not vanished, they had simply gone to ground, maybe until they were brave enough to face us, but this was a long way off.

Bob and me were unpredictable as far as what we did with ourselves.One minute we would be selling scrap metal, then the next we would be trying to look older and taller with our bum fluff moustaches hoping to get picked to go tatty picking and thrown on the back of a lorry like immigrants at Calais for a fiver a day at 04:00 in the morning, or camping out in the garden and grabbing an early start to rip off the milkman, well it wasn't the milkman it was the householder.You see, we never pinched the milk off doorsteps, we had it boxed off, our scam was so much more advanced.After selecting the houses we would leave a note in the empty bottle left for milky, the note would tell milky exactly what we wanted, bread, fresh orange, eggs and then we would wait like snipers, collect our loot before the cunts woke up.Who gives a fuck who paid the bill this was our landand this was their stealth tax to pay, it was still all about growing.Extra scrambled eggs on toast with fresh orange whilst staring at your little biceps willing them to get bigger, that's what it was about.

"ALL THE PROCEEDS OF THIS BOOK ARE GOING FOR MINE AND DAVE'S SESH IN ISAAC WILSON'S".

Dave

4

Teesside

There was always a time this malarkey would stop and Bob and me would move on to bigger things we're getting too old for this shit, smart clothes and combed hair, with my big brothers aftershave freshly stolen from his room while he was out shoplifting.He knew but he was the best brother you could wish for, he was the business.My bro was a tough guy, a real one, one of the ones I spoke about earlier, you just can't find people like him anymore, he was all of five foot six, covered in an assortment of shit tattoos, borstal dots and female names scattered about his arms and legs and they only made sense to him.With scars all over his body each one telling a different story, of a different battlefield, he never bothered with the gym or fitness, he was a natural, his fists, anger and ability came from his heart and was the kind of man you could never beat no matter who you were. Frank was the man that would always go one step further than his enemy.

Then there is Norman, the oldest, he was doing hard time for firearms offences. Norm was like a clone of Frank, together, wherever they were there was double trouble, bad news for the opposition that's all I can say. Norm and Frank even looked alike and scrapped like lions, I remember a time Frank and Norm walked into a flat, Frank's best mate Chris was already there, I will tell you about Chris later. Chris was waiting with two young lads Frank hadn't seen before, Frank gives Norm the nod, "these alright kid?" he asks politely, Frank was always polite. Chris was swift with his reply, "yea kid they're sound don't worry" that was good enough for Frank, he pops out a shotgun and lays it on the table like a placemat.After a short chat they left, and one of the young lads who sat watching, trying to be invisible runs to the front door to throw up, "go on kid get it out" Norm slaps him on the back to help him feel better along with laughing at the poor chap.

Frankie and his pals were priceless, with each one having their own version of what Frankie meant to them. So, there was one friend of his, he went by the name little Chris, I would like to say he was worth his weight in gold but that wouldn't be heavy enough, you see Chris was about the same size as me n Bob and we loved him for that.He was all of five three, again covered in tattoos that looked like some artist hated him and wanted to practice, but do not be fooled by his size, that got him into more scrapes than anyone over the years and what he didn't have in size he made up for with his heartand loyalty to his friends.He would carve you like a Toby no matter who you were, he was the firework of the bunch, the kind of guy you could trust without questioning.A mean these people are relics in Teesside these days, antiques, nowadays shitbags just want to keep themselves out of prison and on the streets living the life, no matter what that costs, you see if all these people have to spend is their friends freedom then it will be spent, like a child with a fiver in the arcades, whilst ringing the loyalty out of the friendship like a wet tea towel, with not a care for where the water landed, after all it can be mopped up. The place was rife with king pin male and female drug lords, running around like cheap versions of Pablo, and I mean cheap by the way, sleeping with the drug squad officers in exchange for what? Their soul maybe, selling nasty to the undead with not a care in the world, or of the damage it may cause. Sending people to jail with no repercussions seemed to be the norm for some around here, people simply pass comment and get on with their lives.I remember a house getting painted black all because the policeman called the lady inside by her first name, these were rules that were never written or spoken you just knew they existed, a bit like the Ten Commandments, back then the town adopted the "I'm Spartacus" way of life, now it's just "he fucking did it".

Battles were often won and lost in the nightlife on a weekend, when you counted all your illicit earnings that you made through the week to buy that shit shirt that was going to be ripped off your back by some fucking fat doorman as he threw you down the stairs, having a scrap was part of the night out, like getting that takeaway on the way home, or giving the taxi driver a hard time as he attempts to bargain with you over the fare, but these scraps were often fair and would result in a black eye or a few stitches.These days you can guarantee a gang of ten thousand will drive a cowardly four by four through your window with no one at the wheel.

The place had regular bobbies that actually ran around the estate like Starsky and Hutch!There was this copper who broke all the fucking rules, he would chase you on your scrambler in reverse top speed, with not a fuck given, his name was Derick, Police Constable had the estate on the run.There's an interesting story about this cunt I will tell you, about when he was a wild one, ruthless and every bit as bent as a butchers hook.He was sleeping with one of the local scallys, little Chris and Frank got right up his nose.He collared Chris one day, thought he could shake him down, like DenzelWashington's 'training day'.After Chris reminded him that he was being a naughty boy going in to see her in number twenty four, "tut tut" laughed Chris. "Listen you forget about all this and I will get off your back, it's your mate I want, Frankie, he's causing us all a real headache." Carta moaned on and on, slipping Chris his number like a fat donut eating, Macintosh wearing detective on a stakeout, thinking he was doing him a favour, Chris laughed, crumpled up the number like an old betting slip that had just let him down for five hundred quid and threw it right back in his face, "fuck you" scowledChris.

Carta never quite got over this, he made it his mission to clean up the streets like some rogue western sheriff wearing a poncho and standing on the edge of town, or like a really shit Robocop, with one hand in his own dirty pocket. Even though he was part of the dirt he was relentless in his pursuit of the criminal, this bastard arrested Frankie for pinching three Rolex's, but only charged him with the theft of one, yes you do the maths, a great Christmas for Carta that year, I did say he was a ruthless cunt didn't I?

Carta would often be seen chasing people through houses, out of windows, right behind them.In them days the police wore a shirt and trousers, with the tie stuffed in their pockets, with a licence to kick your fucking head in, nowadays Bobbies look like they're going into battle, on call of duty ps4, with the shit they carry they couldn't run a bath. Police brutality was common, often when the van turned up to lock someone up, half a dozen would climb in the back, just to make sure the prisoner was comfortable and his needs were met.We never had mobile phones to record the moments that shook the vehicle like an earthquake and so out they would come one after another looking deshelled, "you lot fuck off" was probably the greeting, and you usually just did in fear of getting thrown in there too.Accept on one weekend when the law grafted hard and filled the van like it was collecting bodies for the rubbish tip outside rumours nightclub, then just as it was full and ready to go to the warehouse, Chris came from nowhere and opens the back doors, setting everyone free, somehow managing to undo a nights work in about ten seconds, now that was a disheartening moment for the boys in blue. To be fair you didn't mess with the police like people do today, they just beat you up, or got someone else to come and pay you a visit on their behalf. This was common practice, I once witnessed a couple of Teesside's finest knocking on the front door of one of Teesside's finest toe rags for a quick chat about a discrepancy concerning a crooked cop.Luckily he wasn't home but the message was relayed to a handful of shitbags on the front step. Hard to believe isn't it, or maybe not. The same kid was beaten half to death three weeks later in broad daylight with a baseball bat, all seven stone of him.

Yes policing was very different back then. A copper once bullied my dear mother like a coward telling her "give me Frankie, or I will take everything with a plug on it", Mother wasn't afraid she would just reply with "oh beat it catch him yourself".

All this was pure education to me and Bob, we had access to all the latest news on who was who and what shitbag did what, we just sat back like a couple of students and listened to all these hero's talk, yea we were like sponges, this is how we learned the trade, this is how we became afraid of nothing or no one, we would stand 12 years old taking mental notes on what these legends were saying, like academics giving lectures with sound knowledge. There was me and Bob saying nothing, then occasionally getting chased out of the room because there was only so much we were allowed to hear if you get me. We loved being around these guys we felt safe, we were learning it all for free. Every now and then one of them would spend a little time in her majesty's hotel, it didn't matter what for, or even if they were the ones that were guilty, it was like a roll call, their turn for the team, while the others got on with the job and shared out the V.O's amongst each other.It was always a pleasure to visit a brother and smuggle what you could into the place, ganja, tablets or whatever to make life more comfortable, after all, it was their turn next.

It was always a sad time when my bro had his turn but he accepted it with honour knowing his pals were right there for him.That is a fantasy these days, you go away,you're on your own and the wings and landings are crawling with shit bags, zombies snorting Subutex or smoking spice breakdancing on the cell floor and being videoed on a mobile phone to upload to social media all to block out the pain. Back then it was like meeting up with old friends, pats on the back and "what you done this time kidda?" shouted from the lifer that sees you quite often and knows you by name, he gives you a big welcome home to get you settled in.

This was only a short-term victory for Carta and his mob, but I imagine a breather was needed now and then, these boys could be slippery bastards and one wrong move from the boys in blue would have the lads back on the streets in no time.

There was a time five CID Bobbies came knocking on our door, "can we come in, thanks" said DC gobshite, as he barged his way past one after another making their way into the front room, "where's Frankie, we just want a quick chat with him?" grinned the same big fella, who brought his gang, each one wearing shit casual untrendy clobber with an old wooden truncheon that sported a leather ponytail at the back end poking out of their jackets. I just remember thinking it was a good job our kid leaped through the window moments earlier, bastards always beat him up in their numbersbut Frank never complained, it was an occupational hazard.He knew he couldn't take on the biggest gang in the country, so he would have to resort to keeping them busy, by staying on his toes.

You see Frank had more friends than the entire police force had put together.His friends stretched the country, real friends, people don't know how to spell friends these days, but there are still old fossils lingering around that still have the same values and beliefs, diamonds in the rough or needles in the haystack.

Even back then whoFrank knew to be friends turned out to be the biggest rats of them all.A mean, the story goes, Frank was locked up in Durham and Chris was on his way in, there had been a rumble in the town with some arse wipe bully, they always get what's coming in the end. Chris did what he does best and put his arse on the line for everyone else with not a thought for himself or the consequences, it's true he was no stranger to her majesty's hotel and knowing your sidekick was already in there with open arms must of been a boost.Chris is marched along corridors, to the clinking sound of keys and iron doors being slammed, shouting and screaming that echoes right through your soul, the door opens "in you go Everton" whispers one of the screws with a friendly nudge and Chris looks around then he looks up, standing way up top arms outstretched was a familiar face it was Frank, standing there with some bloke called Duffy. "Chris" shouts Frank at the top of his voice, it echoed all the way down to ground floor.Chris smiles and punches the air "yes, my man Frank" Chris bellowed like he wanted everyone to know, with a smile that made him two foot taller, at that moment they knew this spell was goanna be ok, they had each other, it's moments like this that last only seconds, yet you find yourself talking about them for a lifetime.

So, they got on with their time which had its moments.There was this Geordie kid who was put in with Frank, was a bit of an idiot and full of himself, wanting to show Frank and Chris how to fight. "Howay man stand up al show ya how tee box" he ordered Frank to his feet. Chris and Frank had been laughing about him all day and how they would deal with him all day.Whispers had crept to the pad that this Geordie was a nonce and that did not sit right with either Chris or Frank. "Ok show me am I doing it right?" Frank replied putting his hands up to his face in an attempt to look like he was hopeless, "nah man ya doing it all wrong" the Geordie replied with a touch of disappointment, he took hold of Franks hands and positioned them for him, "reet man hold it there" laughed this Geordie, "like this?Am I ok now?" Frank is now square on to this fucker and Chris is laughing like fuck from the top bunk, "how's that?" said Frank,then let go the fastest right hand you ever did see, whack, the Geordie falls to the ground and Chris and Frank well, you can imagine. That nonce was moved off the wing within the hour, makes you think why the screws had put him on there to start with, or even with the two fireworks from Middlesbrough.

Frank made some great friends with lads from all over the country, he wasn't precious to 'boro' only he accepted you as a person, I recall a story that was typically him. There was a big guy called Miller from Sunderland, he was a gentleman and thought very highly of Frank, he knew he would back him on the inside with anyone because Frank saw that quality in their friendship.A few people didn't like this comrade, that bloke Duffy who was there at the same time as Frank, at some point they were pals, but this guy had his own demons, he wanted to take over Miller and the makems and whatever they were up to.Well loyalty was Frank's thing and he wasn't a bully, he disagreed with this fella Duffy and so stood by his friends which was to be costly to Frank a few years later. Duffy was moved and so the stretch continued.

On the outside things were to take a grizzly turn, a friend of Frankie's had been brutally murdered, she was the mother of a small child and was a really good friend of the family.She was senselessly stabbed to death in her own home.It took police months to find the man that did it, but when they did, he never planned on being put right in the same prison or even the same wing as Frank, as you can imagine this was a stroke of luck and a bit of karma for this bastard. With a smashed chair leg Frank set about him hurting him badly, he bounced this fucker all around his pad, blood everywhere, he bashed his face and his eyes, after he was finished and before the screws got to him, he kneeled down to his lifeless body and whispered, "you will never look at another beautiful woman in your life," then he was carted off the block with a sense of great satisfaction, I mean what else could he do for a dear friend.

The Club...

We were in the best company growing still thinking we were smashing enough protein and not needing to do much else, occasionally playing around with the dumbbells that were never used, at times re-enacting the stories amongst ourselves. The local youth club was a good hang out, but we never told anyone anywhere that we were coming, it always gave us the advantage, less these cunts knew the better. In these places, it was a chance to show our faces and let the local bacteria know we were game as fuck.From a distance, we would just see the disco lights throbbing behind the closed curtains, and the muffled sound of the Jam, or that song "oh Geno" or some other shit. As we got closer to the front door the young smokers would liven up, stump their fags out and pass down the line that Bob and Dave were coming, like a Chinese whisper, by the time it got to the front door it would have been "Bob and Dave are gonna smash the place up," which wasn't true of course, smashing the youth club up was not on our agenda, it would serve no purpose. We were there to shake up the crew who was running the joint. Standing in the doorway up ahead was a couple of shit bags, then, for about ten metres either side, stood the rats, the ones you could never trust, the ones that would always lay the boot in, you had to watch these mongrels from the side because these were the ghosters, experts at it. Bob is straight onto it lunging forward sharply "what the fuck are you looking at?Al snap ya jaw ya daft cunt." "Noone mate" winced the little chubby kid as he lit up a ciggy. "I am not your fucking mate al punch your fucking head in," Bob wanted to go ahead there and then, I think he forgot what we were here for, "Bob, Bob, fuck sake man howay" I ushered him away from this porky little fucker, I done him a favour really but that was never acknowledged.

We are yards from the front door, and as we get closer the building feels like it is surrounding us, and the door is getting smaller, each shit bag briefly making eye contact and giving us a nervous nod then looking away like they haven't seen us, with more ghosts in their hands than the whole of SouthfieldRoad.Up ahead there is a couple of germs we haven't seen before, which makes it better for us, I need to get us in peacefully but Bob wants to smash these two standing in our way. "Awright shouts Bob, what's the score in here?" The two lads look at each other, "what the fuck you looking at him for? Al punch your fucking head ya mong." Bob is seriously up for it, "take it easy lad" with arms outstretched one of them mutters, they know who we are, the Chinese whispers got to them long before we did, there was a bit of silence then after ten seconds the taller one of the two opened the door, "get yourselves in lads" he mumbled, "fucking right we're going in, eh you wha, eh?" screamed Bob.At this point am pulling him by the arm into the club, "come on leave it man." We both re-adjusted our Harrington jackets and done a much needed visual sweep of the place, we needed to know who the fuck was in here, Bob is wanting to go to business, I am doing the maths, I am counting heads, who's who, and should we need it, our exit.More importantly, our job was to be in and out sending a really quick message.

Now, we had been making enemies since we were born, even as far back as on the hospital ward, nurses, doctors, other little rats all wanted a piece of us, it felt like that.The youth club was a place they all gathered, bringing their memories with them of Bob and Dave, taxing their bottles of milk then reselling the fucker back to them for double bobble, so fuck you what!

They were all in there in their little huddles, for me this was not safe for us but for Bob, it was right where he wanted us, he said he wanted to punch fuck out every single one of them, he could not of been in a better place right now, his anger levels reaching boiling point, fists clenched, "what do want to drink big lad?" I shouted, my confidence was growing around Bob I was always aware that the bastard could bite, but I was his pal, he knew that. "Coke and a bag of crisps" handing me ten pence, we always went halves, fifty fifty me and Bob even in drama, his trouble was mine and mine his although I rarely started anything.If it was ever my shout for a rumble it would be legit. There is plenty of nodding, "now then lads" and offers of drinks, sweets, and cheap lies but we never forgot the last time these bastards set us up, like a said before no cunt is ghosting us ever again.

At the counter with our plastic cups of rola cola bought from Frank Dee's and shite crisps acquired from doggy market, we needed a safe spot with the wall behind us and not some cheap punk who had been paid a wham bar to throw a ghost by some bacterial shit bag who had a grudge, there was plenty of both here, and plenty of darkness, ideal circumstances for the ghost, in here it was back to back Bob and me against the world, but somehow that's how we liked it.

Bob fancies a game of pool, come to think of it, so did I, it was closer to our target and sent a perfect message of defiance. The pool table area was where you hung out if you were someone, so that's where Bob wanted to be, after all, he was Bob. Already playing were a couple of lads who seemed ok but finished up their game real quick when we arrived, Chinese whispers again I guess.Sat in the corner like a rubbish Scarface in the bubble bath, with two maggots either side was the local boxer, now this cunt was a boxer by default because his Dad was a boxer and his dad before him and so on and so on, he even wore the belcher with solid gold boxing gloves to tell the world 'he did a bit', he was one of Teesside's 'boxer under pressure' if you get me, forced to take up the sport even though he was shit, but he has a job and a reputation to keep, which we kind of respected but then didn't, we just wanted him to know that.

When me n Bob showed up it was always the same response, these termites never knew where to look always waiting for instructions, backless cunts.So, we take over the pool table and make things uncomfortable, adding a little cloud to the atmosphere was what Bob did so well, creating an environment that was uneasy to be in was Bob's favourite pastime, the pool table was perfect for this you could crouch down, your chin on the cue and stare right at your target then take your shot, get up like it meant nothing leaving a paranoid taste in their mouth, we were here for a rumble but we were completely outnumbered and the clever bit was that we were the only ones that knew it, we needed to have the poker face if that makes sense.

"Two shots Bob" I shouted "oh really" muffled bob, as he laughed which was rare because this was a business situation, he passed the cue then like a bolt of lightning threw his two shots at the boxer both hitting their target like a drone strike in Bagdad, all shit bags jump up, I land the perfect shot with the left at an angle, out of nowhere I felt a sharp thump across my shoulders and the sound of wood snapping as the fat part of the spare cue hits the floor, now we know where that other fucking cue was, it was being prepared for my back "arrrgh, ya bastard" I screeched, this fucker dropped me to my knees and fast, this was not a safe place to be I couldn't help but think at this moment we had been set up.This fight was over I needed to think fast and get us out of this situation, it was like an IED had gone off at the roadside and we had to get out of there.After dealing with the dizzy stars in front of my eyes and the rib shot that took my breath away, I could barely make out where Bob was, he was still on his feet trading shots for fun but foolishly he was wearing a hoodie and one of the maggots had hold of him like a dog on a lead, with blurred vision my only job was to throw shots and bail this nightmare with my pal, we never leave a man down.

By now the adult staff had intervened and rescued us from what can only be described as our first defeat, fat lips and keggys, but you know what, we had never laughed so much in our lives, "fuck sake Bob what the fuck happened there you were supposed to take out that little shite hawk" I said in-between coughing and shaking my head, "fuckoff you know I did him, I know I did" he laughed because he knew this was a lie, to be fair Bob had three to deal with, I had one and one sneaky cunt from behind, you see this is Teesside in full swing, younglings growing and copying parental behaviours, you can't take on a somebody without taking on his crew. So, with an arm round Bob for support we limped up the street keeping the funny side of what happened in the conversation.That moment was like a brotherhood moment, I knew that I could always count on this little bastard and he could always count on me no matter what, you cannot buy that these days sadly, but back then it was earned.Tonight we learned a lesson about trust, a lesson about the kind of people that lived amongst us and smiled at us in the park, all wearing masks hiding their insecurities and weaknesses forever.

There were many more of these confrontations in our early teens, and we never lost many scrapes and tracking down shitbags individually was a trick we learned really quickly.Hard to believe that boxer, who with his pals traded shots with Bob in the youth club, was quick to piss his pants when we found him alone on the tarzi over the beck, same story today really, you see I was never without Bob, and Bob was never without me.

The taste for it...

Early teens were all about sitting back watching and learning as much as we could about whatever was going on. The world was our lecture theatre and the bigger idiots were our tutors.Me and Bob, at this stage, were sat at the back of the class not saying much but always taking notes, that was pretty much our senior school, watching the tough guys squabbling over who was the best fighter in the school n all tha and who had the prettiest girl n all tha

Things always seemed to reverse in life, like the girl that was gorgeous in school and hung off the best fighters arm, now has four kids a coke habit and hair extensions straight off the horses tail, living in some shithole with the same guy who was once Maximus and now struggles to get home from a Sunday afternoon in the local club with his pot belly and his re-told tales of 'when I was', that people are sick of hearing.

So, thats how growing up happened really, all the tough guys become shitbagsand well, you get what am saying.

Me and Bob liked to be sort of middle of the range here, we weren't the tough guys in this school of bigger people but we certainly were not the runt of the litter, we simply got left alone if there were any bullying going on. I think there was an invisible CV that arrived before we did, it was read by all, with unspoken mutual nods, and the occasional "awright" would be exchanged, we often wondered if the teachers were in on this because at times even they would pass comments like "oh so you are the young Mr Taylor", I thought this was special but really they had been hassled by all my older brothers before me and this was their way of letting me know and maybe preparing themselves for a rough ride.

We eased our way through the ranks, we never wanted that title of hardest in the school bullshit, although Bob often would find himself fantasising about punching the fucking head in of Gonzo the top boy, he would always tell me how he would easily take that cunt out, as his psychiatrist I would always advise against.

So, schools would clash on the field over the beck, this was a real opportunity for the tough nut to earn his pay against the other tough nuts of the other schools. I mean this was a battle none of them wanted to lose but everyone wanted to win.So, in true Teesside fashion, these fights never really got off the ground, it was better just to talk about how close it was to happen, pretty much the same as today to be fair, that way the shitbags could add their usual seasoning and a touch of spice, in favour of their man of course.

Me and Bob seen this from a distance and would laugh when the fight got "called off" I mean this was our neck of the woods, a rumble one on one or whatever, three on one blah blah, you see we always laughed after a scrap and moved on.There was a real-life actual fight on the school field with the "second best fighter" and the other schools "second best fighter" I mean who the fuck is in charge of rankings anyway, how does that even work? This scrap was not going our man's way and the performance was nothing short of poor, our man was one of the many Teesside boxing elite that I spoke of earlier and he wasn't doing so good, me and bob looked at each other and shook our heads in dismay, then Bob laughed and shouts "I am gonna help him out", "no no wait Bob fuck sake" I shouted but he was off.Through the crowd Bob wades pushing people out the way, he steps up to the pair of "second best fighters" holds his arms out to both chests, in a gesture to stop the fight like some gypsy referee demanding fair rules at Appleby fair.I have to just stand and watch close by so I have his back, both lads heavy breathing our guy is beat, the other kid wants to finish him like they do in that arcade game Street Fighter. Bob drops his shoulder, waits, then snaps a left hook out ending the fight like a bullet to the head. Bob takes no credit for this, he didn't like the fuss and so mingled back into the crowd and out at the arse end, we did our obligatory laugh and waltzed back into the yard like nothing had happened.Well nothing did to be fair, our second-best fighter kept his title, and he had a deep respect for Bob and me after this, like an unsaid thank you, with a pass that got us everywhere with everyone, we never quite understood how the pecking order was monitored, or who by, it was indeed pure bullshit created by the very people that were involved, a bit like politicians do these days, it was just funny to watch and hear the stories told.

So, with this unspoken respect, we had the freedom of the school, freedom to sell what we wanted without repercussion, people just seemed to leave us alone, it was how we liked it, we just wanted to make our coin and bail at the end of the day.Cigarettes was where it started we knew there were mugs out there willing to pay forty pence for a single fag, we did the maths and by the end of the day, cash was flowing.We never held the merchandise just the money, it was smooth we gave the nod, distribution and handling would come from different people, clockwork stuff.

Bob rarely had to dish out discipline when it come to our goods, we introduced chocolate into the sales and money was not an issue, we even had a tic list that was written in code obviously, code only me and Bob would ever understand. This went on for many years, hassle free, even sold goods to the teachers but that's another story, like Mr White we had these fuckers sewn up.

It was on the way home one afternoon that I was to sense something in Bob that was to become who we were, a moment I can always look back at and say, that's where this shit all began, in that very moment. Under instructions to collect some stamps on the way home for my Mother, we called in at the local post office.Now, this was a simple everyday task, go in buy stamps and leave with no intrusive thoughts or goings on, I stopped for a moment to catch this fucking lunatic staring at the post office sign, his underdeveloped mind thinking, which was unusual for him, "Bob, Bob what the fuck are doing"? I shouted in a whisper, he stood looking at his watch, and counting, then turned to face the counter, counting some more, before walking outside still staring at his watch, then as the two security guards walked out with empty cases, he stopped his clock, then stared some more, the whole thing was bizarre to watch. "Bob!" I snapped him out of his trance, standing there with a book of stamps "the fuck was that?" I asked. Bob started to visualise which was a common trait of this little psychopath, the guard made eye contact with him, Bob gestures in a mime the discharging of a firearm, the guard shook his head in disbelief and shouts " go on clear off ya little cunt" I still didn't get it, "imagine how much cash was in them cases" laughed Bob, "yea you're off your fucking rocker you" I chortled, "come on let's get off home" I said calmly.

I wanted to change the subject because I had a very strange feeling in my tummy, Bob however, he walked backwards, glaring at the post office like it had just shit in his kettle and there was a moment I thought I saw Bob holding an invisible shotgun at his waist, I knew it was a shotgun, his hands were close together and this would be the weapon of choice for him, but that was my thoughts not his,I mean I could be wrong about the whole thing.This violent little cunt appeared to have a bit of a penchant for post offices and was fulfilling some fantasy that we had already lived out in the bedroom many years ago with his poor little sister and her rag doll. A disturbing mind or just a teenager who liked violence, and control? Fucking both, my psychiatric skills were to be tested here, how was I ever going to put this right? Maybe I wasn't meant to, this was who he was and by default, it was who I was to become also. I was his pal and he was mine that was never questioned, this is the basics we learned from the older brothers and his motley crew, that your friends are your friends and that loyalty should never be questioned, why would you need to, it was like a way of being loyal and being loyal was like being human, it was who you were.

Loyalty...

Today what does that word even mean, people round these parts would fuck your girl for the sake of it, then "swear down dead a never" til the cows come home.Loyalty is a gift that if you have it, then we want to know you, you can't learn this shit it's not something that you can lie on a CV about or even pretend to have in the short term.It is a fine quality and it runs through your veins like the blood you carry, you should never need to test your friends' loyalty, you should already know that it exists. I have always known about my big stupid Bob's and he never doubted mine, this was clear.This gift was genetic and then re-enforced by years of watching and learning from the folk who put it into practice more than anyone.When you see real loyalty in action against the shit bag behaviour of today's rats, it's emotional, it brings a grown man to tears but the tears are allowed, they confirm a bond like no other.

There can be no greater sacrifice than to give your freedom, when a Teesside shoplifting squad, as described in the local paper, hit Cumbria with what was "a rampage of villainy" in a northeast crime wave, gets a pull on the way home.With Teesside in their sights, one man in a car full of Middlesbrough's finest crooks and most wanted with a full days loot in the boot in true 'I'm Spartacus' bravery, is insistent that everything in the car belonged to himand everyone else had nothing to do with how it magically got there.With not an eye batted, this wasn't a pre-arranged agreement by the way, it just so happened that he spoke up first, that man was my brother, it was his turn and everyone did not feel the guilt like you might expect, what they felt was loyalty and Frankie knew this would be at a cost of eighteen months from his lifespan, but it was his turn, he was looked after and so was our Mother. I can't think of a more purer example of loyalty. After witnessing this at this level, our young DNA was really taking shape.

Bob was always a cunt but we looked for opportunities to practice this way of being.When the police turned up at my house, yea you guessed it, "Carta", for a stolen motorbike we were chased on that day, Bob stepped forward square on to Mother with a poker face that was so full of shit you could smell it, and took the hit, "it was me Mrs T, Dave wasn't even there," and before I could get a word in, he would give me that look, that look that said "shut your fucking mouth" Mother knew this was bullshit, if Bob was there then so was her boy and she raised her eyebrows, with a slight shake of the head and a silent narrow of the eyes, she understood the code and gave a look backthat spoke a thousand words, something like "well done Bob but you're both in my shit book." You see Mother was a well-respected and well liked member of the community, she knew how all these little gangsters operated, you couldn't lie to her she always knew, she had heard all the possible combinations of bullshit that could ever be told. At that point I realised it was his turn and so just like the stories we heard this was fucking real, it felt solid, Bob was in the shit and I wasn't, but hey he was goanna cash his cheque in at some point when it was my turn, that's how it was.

Like the time Frank got himself into a serious situation with a knife and a bully in the town centre and the way out of this tricky situation was stabbing himself twice in the leg, then climbing into bed until the next day when mother pulled back the covers back to a pale human in the foetal position "what the fucking hell has happened here" Mother screamed at him, it was like a scene out of Halloween, he was really lucky that day he needed blood, a hospital bed and when the news came on the television he needed to hand himself in too, on Mothers orders. This shaved several years off the lifespan. Instead of eight years he was sentenced to two years and the circumstances around what happened were typically Frank, he intervened when this bully was beating up a friend half his size, this shit bag pulled a knife on Frank which then sent him into 'it's me or him mode', in this predicament you do or die and Frank was not ready to go.

If you ever want to highlight loyalty this would be a moment for that.

On a more personal note, I recall a time me and Bob smoked one too many spliffs and turned white, then had to walk through the living room past a thousand faces, all staring at me in slow motion. "what the fuck has happened to him?" shouted Mother, "you stay there Mam, I will go and see" offered Frankie with a huge grin on his face, he burst out laughing when he walked into the kitchen, this bastard knew what the problem was, he was in hysterics, "shh he said unable to contain his laughter, "quick get a drink of water and eat this", he handed me some chocolate, "you have been smoking haven't you?" he asked, a little more serious this time, "don't tell our mam Frank" I begged him, he would never tell her, he just looked at me let out another laugh, and winked "finish that drink al sort it."Frank was the best at reassuring me, I heard him shout to Mother "he's alright Mam." I couldn't help but feel like this was a moment I was never going to forget like Frank had me over a fucking barrel, nightmare, but true to his word he sorted it and yes this story always came up at my expense.

So, as we were growing up we were collecting a tool bag of life skills, tools that most shitbags on this rock couldn't afford let alone acquire, what we needed to do was ditch the bag and make the tools part of who we were, we don't carry a tool bag these days, the qualities, become our very way of being, we had plenty of time for this, we were still learning remember at an alarming rate, both me and Bob often would reminisce about Smigga and his disloyal team of cowards that day in the playground, you can bet your arse these fuckers are as untrustworthy today as they were back then.

Finding our temple...

Amidst all the learning and brawls, and the strange post office fantasies that still haunt me, we never forgot that growing, and consuming protein was top of our list, we thought it was enough to eat a tin of tuna in the afternoon ad hoc, for no reason we needed to up our growing game.At the moment all we had was an old punch bag with black tape holding it together in the shed that got some stick off Bob every day and the old five kilogram dumbbells that look like they were made in a blacksmiths shed by some old farrier.Our training routine would consist of me on the bag, Bob curling the dumbbells and shadow boxing with a few sit-ups.

We have been trying to grow since we came into this place and our tool bag is looking impressive, we were angry little bastards with good compasses, we were still learning from what we perceived to be as the "best", this is the point where we become "game as fuck."

As for careers, well there is only one job for little cunts like us, we were focused on being scaffolders, that laddish collection of shit tattoo bearing tough guys, that wear their hard hats on backwards and tell the health and safety wanker on site to fuck off!We never realised tilt we bailed the idea, that this breed was unique, like carbon copies of each other, a family of real men who fart in their hand and throw it in your face like a baseball in a yank stadium, accept that fucker.Make the advanced a brew and you will be on to your part two in no time and when this lot got together on a night out, well that's another ball game, clones stinking of creed and wearing gold for fun.

After bailing that fucking idea, the next one that we would become, what everyone else in Teesside is, a cage fighter!This idea didn't last long, we couldn't cope with the dead ferret hair doo that you needed to have to qualifyand the constant strolling through the town in a mood growling at folk, with the low slung 'tap out' gym bag, banging off the ankles and the hand wraps that never get taken off, even in costa after the gym sesh, simply wasn't our bag.This look was for the likes of Jones and Khanage, getting cuddles, rolling and being tea bagged in the octagon by a semi-naked hairy fat bastard with cauliflower lugs did not flick our switch. Having a boss telling us what to do didn't seem to fit our way of working.

At sixteen me and Bob got a job with this roofer, he was ok I suppose, we needed to try something I guess, he was alright really he thought he was funny but his banter was shit, anyway cut a long story short we kicked his fucking head in and threw him off some scaffolding, cheeky cunt called Bob a "young Doyle", roofing wasn't our thing, we weren't into ripping pensioners off.

We tried plastering with this little fat bastard called Brett he was ok like, bit of a gobshite, got right on Bob's tits one day talking about this and that, Bob shouts at him "shut your fucking fat mouth, ya getting on my wick" cunt thought he could backchat Bob, no that isn't happening so Bob punched his fucking head in and we both got the sack.

The only thing left on this rock was what we avoided the most, well I did anyway but Bob was always drawn to it, even back in the day on the beach when we first met he would reach for the sea, yea that's right the offshore rigger, now this bunch were raw and pure Teesside, I mean you cut an offshore man in half, and what you get is red and white, ICI, town hall, Staffordshire bull terriers, Chubby Brown, Chris Rea, and last but not least a parmo running right through the middle. This bunch shout from the rooftops, in a tone only the scaff can understand, "I work offshore doenna." They drive their unnecessary four wheel drives around the council estate never needing to test that four wheel differential, buying magazines about bigger wheels, stereos and bumpers, they tuck their motors into bed with a pillow behind the wrought iron gates, on the driveway of the house tarted up like DannyLe Roux, that is protected by the two concrete lions standing proudand has more CCTV than the Cleveland Centre.Sporting the biggest plasma on the estate is what it's all about, today these lads post their pictures, wearing all the gear, orange overalls, hard hats, and safety harnesses just in case they missed anyone, oh and you may get the obligatory helicopter in the background shot, it wasn't uncommon to hear them drop the infamous phrase "am back away next week arna" and with their WAG's in tow, who may as well be on the platform too, with their knowledge of "our lad and choppers eve", with their wardrobes a plenty, and small business on land to keep them busy, funded by the trillionaire rigger.They are a priceless bunch and we love them dearly, they're a solid bunch with real pubes on their balls and chest hair like a silverback, together with the scaff they are a force, badgering the Aberdeen train and its 'normal' passengers into huffing and puffing for the whole thousand hour journey. Bob loves it, the whole fighter pilot status, but it wasn't my bag and right now, what we actually worked out, was we needed to be our own boss so that's what we set out to do.

It was taking its time working out what we wanted, so in the meantime, we were like little mini versions of our lot. Walking in town and planning our first job, a job that would earn us something was a regular occurrence, half the time it was fantasy talking but we had the balls for anything, all we needed was the opportunity.

For some unknown reason we were stopped in our tracks, "lads give us a hand with this stock will ya" said this voice from nowhere, we turned and there stood a tank, a giant, Bob with his usual charm fired back "eh, who yatorken to, what's it worth?" It was like he didn't give a fuck. Bob was locked into negotiations with a giant in a vest, fuck sake we couldn't take this cunt on but I was in the stance and so was Bob, "chill lads, give me a hand al give you's a free week upstairs" he said back with look of disbelief that two skinny youngsters were about to take him down and attempt to punch fuck out of him. We agree to help him without even knowing what a free week upstairs even was. So we grab a box each and head upstairs with this big cunt, we can hear music, and the clinking clattering sounds of heavy steel being slammed on the floor, "what the fuck?" moaned

Bob.As the door opened we froze, jaws dropped, "you fucking beauty" this place was called 'Steel City' I mean could you think of a better fucking name, it was a temple to worship the steel. I looked straight at Bob and at the same time we both shouted, "we're fucking home." This place was the biggest fucking house of steel we had ever seen, people lifting a thousand ton in one go, "this fucking place Dave" Bob slapped my chest and that tank ushered us in, "have a look around boys and al sign you up, come get ya fucking scrawny arses in" he laughed.

This place fell into our laps, we were meant to find this fucking house of pain, we mooched about the place row after row of steel, dumbbells a crane couldn't lift. Thousands of machines and the stench of zero carbs, we took a left and followed the wall into a room that had bags in all shapes and sizes hanging off the ceiling, "we really are home Bob" I laughed and Bob joined in, it was like we had found treasure. After a while the tank shouted us back to the counter "lads over here, let's get you two some muscles, I'm Mick by the way I own the place," he giggled as he ruffled up Bobs hair "come back tomorrow start your week then and we will sort you out."

This was to be our new home for the rest of time, we went back the next day right on time, we got our free week and Mick showed us around, this is where the training started.Mickwas good to us but we didn't give a fuck about anything, that bag room was to become our home.Walking in there and seeing gangs of shit bags using the bags to practice the ghost shot was quite alarming, we often would catch people staring at one, then under their breath mutter "what did you just say to our lass?" before his pal would ghost the bag from a different angle.It sounds funny but these vermin were like raptors, this shit wasn't our thing. Bob would always stroll in "are you ladies finished on that fucker?" In the stance ready to go, "yea sound" some unidentified coward would squeak from nowhere, "well yea is sounda said it was sound didna" Bob threw back the reply, I stepped in with "go on then fuckoff" all walking

66

backward not a bead of sweat amongst them, Bob adds "go on, fuck off". These moments were common and we had respect for Mick the tank, we never wanted to upset him although a did think Bob was goanna take the gym off him at one point but that's another story.For now, we all got along well. Bob often commented on how Mick waltzed around like he owned the place, Bob sized everyone up.

Our encounters with the law were becoming more frequent, they could never catch us but always knew we were involved.A run in with Carta was enough to put you off graft for good, but Bob always wanted to take on this wanker head on and if Bob was head on, then so was I.

Leaving the gym one night and the smell of green was like a gravy trail, "it's getting stronger Dave" Bob whispers as his nose is pointing in the air, "over here Bob" I am like a springer spaniel by this time, then we bumped into a couple of kids on the corner,these two little fuckers looked as shifty as politicians handing in expense receipts, now these could see we were on the green trailand without a thought of who we might be "psst you want green bro?" Whispered one of the kids through his cupped hand and a hooded head. Bob was on edge, if there was dosh nearby he would sniff it out, but I needed to control the next part of this deal before Bob bulldozed in, "what's the score mush, what you got?"I asked him but we had no intention of handing over money, out of the corner of my eye his pal, moved a large bin and a manhole cover, daft cunt just revealed his stash. Bob was thinking what I was thinking, for the first time we were on the same page, "how much you got"? These kids were brand new, "we will pop back later about ten fella" I whispered in a friendly voice, we didn't want to spook these two idiots.We shook hands, and pulled these two into our friend zone, temporarily of course.

Now, this wasn't our usual thing but fuck it in for a penny and we might get a good score. I was all about turning up with a bat and grabbing this green on a scooter, Bob he wanted to smash these fuckers first, I didn't see the point but how could I stop him? We always had a scooter handy and our Frankie always had spare balaclavas, so we were all set, the plan was simple, twenty seconds tops. I always did everything by the clock and Bob always ruined it.

We pull up, Bob is off the back before we have come to a stop, he's throwing shots for fun, he was wind milling before the bike came to a halt, these kids are going nowhere, "fuck sake" I shouted, no names we weren't that stupid, we had learned a lot over the years, I pull the bat out of the front of the scooter and wrap a calf muscle, "get the fucking bag now" I ordered this cunt with the bat under his chin, my Dad was from Glasgow, so a Scottish accent was easy for meand might throw these mugs off the scent. Bob is making a mess of the other kid for no reason really, the bag was handed over and I slapped his face just in case he wanted another go, I was on the bike revving like a Lambretta off Quadrophenia. "Let's Nash, fucking leave him" I shouted in a whisper, Bob is in no rush at all he's still pounding this cunt like a cheap steak, after about a thousand years he walks calmly away from them both and just before mounting the scooter, points at the terrified youth and says "al punch your fucking head in, eh you what?" "Get on ya mad cunt" I wasn't fucking about now we were 20 seconds over our time, I wasn't happy but we're off laughing like fuck all the way back home, balaclavas still on through red lights and on the footpath, if Carta was out and about we were fucked, he would have us clocked in a flash.

Straight up the ally Mam is at the bingo, Dad is in bed, the shed was open, the light was on, "oh fuck", I whispered to myself, we had to get this bike in off the streets and the balaclavas back in Frankie's stash before he knew, "turn the engine off, Bob whispered" just then the shed bursts open, it's Frankie, Chris, and a bunch of others all playing cards "what the fuck?" shouts Frank. Chris is standing there with a samurailike a Boro ninja ready to take us down, me n Bob standing with balaclavas on, shitting it, we rip the headgear off before we're mincemeat, everyone bursts out laughing except me n Bob, "fucksake you two" laughed Chris who was ready like an assassin to chop us up like a leg of lamb, "where the fuck have you been?" Slapping me on the head affectionately, Frank cared too much to upset his brother."These hats need burning kid" he whispered worryingly, so fuck knows what they have been used for. Frank is no idiot, so he's looking at me, Bob, a stolen scooter, a baseball bat lodged in the front, in a makeshift battle on the move pouch, balaclavas half hanging off our heads, with possible DNA from some serious shit lurking on the inside, a bag with two ounce of weed, and three packets of crisps, he just turns to Chris and bellows out the biggest laugh of all and am still thinking about the lie I would need to tell him. I mean he's still my big brother and lying to him was difficult. It all worked out,Chris had put the fucking sword back in its scabbard, Frank was still pissing himself laughing and between them, they coughed up forty quid for the green.Me and Bob had a good night, gym membership for the month and some dosh left over to buy muscle vests. "That was a fucking lucky escape" I muttered quietly, Frank was a lot of things, but he never wanted us in any bother, we respected him for that, it was onto the next score whatever that was.

Away days…

Football was a big part of this lot, away games and Stanley blades, Idon't think this fucking mob knew how to kick a ball, never mind understand the fucking rules, Frankie probably couldn't name a single player on our side.These cunts were in it for the pain, the victory, and am not talking about points. We were never allowed to go to the matches with them, took us years to realise why, but Notts County away was our first taste of what the game was actually about. Amidst all the shit chants of "you'regonna get your fucking head kicked in", and "who are ya, who are ya" from the other side that almost deafened us,I could see Bob's face being re-fuelled with anger like a plug was shoved up his arse, he was being charged up like an old Nokia, this was right up his street and although we were a couple of kids surrounded by thousands of brainless thugs, we wanted some.Glancing over to the left was a rumble, a bloke wearing our colours kicking the shit out of what looked like a twenty year old foetus curled up protecting his bonce.The guy was done but the red scarf kept going, out of nowhere Frankie and a handful of others leap to the dividing fence "fucking leave him alone, let him get up" shouted Frank, he repeated himself again, "ere fucking get off him" he raged, nothing, the kid on the ground was helpless and screamed for his life.Frank climbs the fence and drops to the other side, landing on his feet like superman and is now toe to toe with what was hard to believe, someone on our side. "I fucking told you to leave him alone" he screamed then lunged forward to hand out a flurry of shots, like the cunt was at a food bank, all landing and finishing this one sided bullshit. After helping the kid to his feet he re-joined the team, you see this was Frankie.In that moment it wasn't about colours or sides, it was about fairness and he was a fair bloke that gave fair warning to that bully. As for me and Bob we learnt a valuable lesson from that five minutes.I did say we had the best teachers in the land didn't I? We're learning, growing and fuelling our minds, but what a lesson this was.

The gym was our playground, and it wasn't long before we saw the results, we were actually growing, the bags were being punished, an hour at a time weights getting thrown around like I'd just smashed our lass. We were on a mission, and them balaclavas that should have been burned well, I kept hold of them in case me and Bob ever got cold on a night time, if you get me. For the first time in his life Bob had an idea, which was worth a listen if nothing else, or maybe I underestimated the big cunt, "you know that fucking van that comes round ere on a night time selling shite?" he whispered, am not sure why he was whispering we were in the middle of a field with our trusty stolen scooter parked up. "Why are you fucking whispering you wooden head" I replied letting out a slow nervous laugh. "Well here's the thing, that van sells all sorts of shit that it shouldn't right?" He had a grin on his face I didn't like. "Go on" I said really slowly, I was curious but feeling that tickle in my tummy, "well the owner is a daft cunt and he couldn't phone the police even if he wanted to, if he did al punch his fucking head in" Bob stared at me and the laughing stopped, I was following every word, I knew where this was going but I played dumb because I wanted to hear what this crazy bastard had to say. "Bob he carries a bat on the van, he is about thirty years old and he wears samba, the cunt plays football and can run faster than this piece of shit scooter," I kicked the machine like it had done something wrong like it was its fault it could only do fifty MPH flat out, but this bike had served us well and earned us some poke so I did feel a little guilty, Iwasn't void of emotions, unlike Bob, who was still whispering. The reason he was muttering and talking quietly was only too real. I am looking at him and the reflection of my face in his eyeballs because they were gleaming, my face was a picture, not knowing what this nut case was about to say next. "Look I was in the shed last night and I overheard your Frankie and Chris talking about something" Bob was using his serious tone by now, so that meant I really did have to listen, but I was not comfortable with mixing our shit with Frankie's, "no whatever it is fuck off" I urged Bob to re-think the next part of this. "Look Chris had something rolled up in an old blanket" Bob is staring at me and this was unhealthy, "Bob no", "DaveI know where it is" Bob interrupted me way before I could finish my sentence. "Look the van stops at the top of the street ten-thirty every night all bar Saturday, we pick a night, grab that thing, you ride the scooter, we put it back before Frankie and Chris even know it's gone, all over in ten minutes." The plan was fucking brilliant, I hated to admit that because it pulled me into the job, but I was more afraid of Frank and Chris finding out than the consequences of getting caught on a fucking scooter, that was pinched, carrying a fucking sawn-off shotgun that had just held up a van. I needed time to think about this, if we were to go ahead I would need to tidy up Bob's plan, polish it a bit because, although it was brilliant, it was also Bob's plan and that meant, well you all know already, no hostages, no deaths and no fucker else ever finding out were my only conditions.

A couple of days had gone by and I had been thinking, still shitting myself because now I knew why Bob was whispering, Frankie had ears everywhere, he knew about all sorts of things before they happened and I prayed he did not hear our conversation from a mile away.

The night is set, Sunday, everyone is hungover and having an early night accept me and Bob and the late night takers of the wobbly egg.The scooter is cleaned and I hand Bob some gloves, Bob disappears into the shed where Chris was sat the night before, there was a loose brick bottom right hand corner, he pulls out the brick and reaches inside with skinny arms, "got it" he whispers, he dusts down an old blanket that's tied with mother's twine, he unrolls it like a napkin in a restaurant, clunk, it rolls out onto the table like a knife and fork, Bob stares at it without a single blink. I can see the reflection of two barrels in his wide open eyeballs like it's Christmas morning and we're six years old, it's like he's waited his whole fucking life to touch one.He reaches out and she is cold, he picks it up and couldn't help himself, waving it around like a cowboy with a grin like next doors moggy, he stuffs it down his jacket and lets out one more big breath and climbs on the back of the scooter like it's a stallion.Its ten o'clock and the van is usually on time so the plan is how Bob said it was, only I insisted that this shotgun, was not to be loaded, we hit the van when there is no one around, we get back to mine put the scooter away and everything else until the next day

Remember we always did everything by the clock, it was a bit weird but it's how we were. It is silent, we can't hear a thing it's like a classic horror film outside, mist, lamp posts and the odd bat silhouetting against the moon flying aimlessly around the street, Christ we even heard an owl winging on.The van pulls up and the engine is turned off, all you can hear is "get me some fags" from Pauline who is waiting for her takeaway, he serves a couple of drunken customers in their dressing gowns and slippers that belong to our lad, so we set off, sounding like a hairdryer we pull up alongside the van, which I think used to be an old ambulance, with a strip of Smokey glass across the top, hand painted in Matt white, the bike still running, Bob jumps off, from here on in we're in slow time lapse, bally down, standing there with a smile he says nothing just throws the van man a bag, who catches it by accident, the man on the van laughs out loud, "go on clear off you little bastard" he shouts, this has no effect, Bob pulls out our new pal, slower than ever he snaps her open and Mr van man realises that we're not playing cowboys and Indians, his smile was wiped from his face as he realised the situation.From his pocket Bob pulls out a cartridge in slow motion, whilst at the same time not taking his eyes off the van man, the cartridge slides in, even slower and fits like a glove, he snaps that fucker shut and the click can be heard at the Boro fish bar, Bob widens his eyes, in the background a small dog that never gets let in the house yaps, "fill that fucking bag up, money and fags" Bob orders the van man, who by now has worked out that this little cunt is mental, serious, and above all has a loaded shotgun pointing at his family allowance.The bag is filled in two minutes, van man has almost pissed his pants and so have I, Bob however, calmly placed the bag on his back, unloaded the shooter, climbed back on the scooter tapping me on the shoulder twice, this was my call to floor this little bastard, the bike had never let us down before but I knew that after tonight we had to part our ways, the scooter would have to go. I bolted off and did what I do best have us the fuck out of there, we needed to get back and out of sight, weaving in and around lampposts mounting footpaths, lights out we trickled into the ally.

After getting back to the shed, the balaclavas had to go, the shooter had to be put back exactly how it was taken and Bob needed a fucking de-brief about the cartridge, the cunt broke the rules, that was not the deal, part of me thinks this crazy little bastard wanted to feel that something extra. So far so good, he rolled up the gat just how he found it and placed it back in the hole. We went home and had a sleepless night, Iwasn't worried about the fucking armed robbery we just pulled off or the 10 years each we could get or the fact Bob had shoved a loaded gun in someone's face, no I was more concerned about my brother and his pals finding out.

The next night we said goodbye to the old trusty scooter and balaclava which should have went weeks agoin a ceremony over the beck with a match and a quick prayer, then it was back to the house.

On the way back home I just had a feeling that something was not right, then I could hear the tyre walls of a car cosying up to the curb at 1MPH the sound of rubber on concrete and dusty brakes squeaking bringing an untaxed, uninsured motor to a halt, Idaren't look but I hear a familiar voice shout through an open window, "Dave, Bob" then a whistle, its Frankie and Chris the back door opens and someone shouts "get in lads", now I knew we were safe that was the one thing that I was certain of.As we climbed into the car there was a smell of ganja, stale aftershave and manky takeaway, all three turned and looked right at us, nobody said a word but I quickly wanted to talk shit about anything other than what I actually knew they were going to talk about, "you still got that scooter lads?" Chris asks like a copper, "nah, we sold it Chris, why did you want it?We can get you one if you like" Bob replied calmly to say the least. Bob was good at that, responding quick, but not as good as Frank, "you go out last night kid?" He had the ability to crack half a smile with one side of his mouth, Frank smirked just like the good cop, almost like this was our only opportunity to come clean, but at this point, we weren't even sure what they knew and we had to stick with that. As the pressure was building in the car Frank and Chris began to laugh and I mean laugh, almost like they fucking knew, "right ok here is a fiver go get yourselves some dinner." Chris chucked me a fiver and all three give me and Bob the narrow eye look, we get out of the car with a sigh of relief, we had to get the fuck out of this situation fast, but just as they pull away, Chris opens the window and shouts to Bob sharply "Bob did you put it back where you found it?" Bob without a single thought replies, "yea Chris". The car drives off under laughter and shit reggae music."Fuck sake Bob" I whispered, "well Ididn't know did I fucking hell", moans Bob as he punches thin air. We never fooled them for one minute, they knew from the second they were told about the van that it was us, that fucking robbery had Bob and Dave all over it, our tiny young brains didn't account for the fact that Frank and his lot were career criminals who know the crack.We had a scooter, two young lads, and there can't have been many shotguns on the estate. I did care about them finding out, however, I also felt a talking to was in the post. I hated disappointing Frank, I guess there was a part of me that wanted him to bring me into his game, but that was never going to happen, he knew his world wasn't for us, he knew that whatever direction his life was heading we were never going to be part of it and that was his gift to me, even though back then I couldn't see it.In an overprotective way, he wanted better things for his younger brother, however, he did buzz off me and Bob and how we went about things. Just to round off an already shit day, me and Bob had not even opened the bag we had stashed from the other night, I guess we were trying to forget it happened for a while.

The next day we were kicking a ball in the street, a mean after all we were still teenagers, doing teenage things, in pulls an unmarked police car with Carta at the wheel, this fucker had been to my house loads of times, I knew what he was about and I also knew he was a cunt.There was a rumour that this bastard used to be a rally driver but that was probably started by him, he was like a dog with a bone when he got onto something and he was onto us bigtime.He had a spotty face and no tie like he wrote his own rules. "Here you two, did I see you riding a scooter the other week, am fucking sure it was you two" he casually guessed, "nah Ican't ride a bike said Bob, I'm Catholic, I just go to school" Carta was always quick with his responses, "don't get fucking smart with me yalittle shit, I want that scooter" he was a control freak, he looked at me and with a daft smile on his face whispers, "how's your Frankie doing?Tell him a said hello," "Tell him your fucking self," I have no idea where that came from, but it fell out of my mouth, like some food that was off or like a sour sweet you give your little sister in the pram. Carta leaped out of the car towering over me, grabbing me by the scruff of the neck and whispering "don't fuck with me young Taylor, am goanna have your brother and his mates, now about that scooter, I want it", he released his grip let me breathe and fucked off, mumbling "I will be back." "What a horrible bastard he was" Bob laughed "if he did that to me ad punch his fucking head in," "right-o Bob, righto."

Whether we understood what the fuck we had become or not, it was real, we didn't just pinch a pair of jeans off the line, steal a loaf from the shop or pass on some moody gold, we were armed robbers, let that bastard sink in and no matter how much Bob plays that fucker down, it was the truth and as for that talking too, well man to man Frank just told me to be careful and to think about it next time, I mean this was his way of showing he wasn't best pleased, it was always hard to hear but at the end, he would always give me a hug then it was forgotten and it really was forgotten.

"HOLME HOUSE IS BOB'S HOUSE."

BOB

5

Respect

Through school, we were becoming more and more disconnected with the setup. I would describe us as being 'distant' from the social norms or non-conformant with the robotic school way of life. It wasn't that we were especially difficult we just had a different way of thinking about things, life, rules etc.. but we did always have respect for those that warranted it, one of our best qualities I guess, when you spend time around people who live and breathe respect it's hard not to make it part of who you are.

Early signs of 'I'm Spartacus' attitudes were there, getting caught at the shit school disco smoking a spliff in the toilet by big Joe Tait was not one of our best moves, I never even smoked it was Boband three others, I just happened to be there.When questioned in the staff room it was me and Bob who admitted it letting the other three off scot free.How we laughed at Joe getting all angry and shouting "you two, I don't know what to do with you, why don't you grow up and be like my lad, join the police force", with his hand on his shiny head towering over the top of us like a shit 'fee fi foe fum giant', I mean this bloke was eleven foot and he was a bully, hard to believe I know but it was true. We looked at each other and thought of Carta, that was enough, I mean Joe Tait never really made any sense because 'his lad' was sacked as part of operation lancet many years later, for corruption and that's Cleveland police and Joe Tait for you. We stood our ground with Tait if Bob would have chinned him I would have followed up with two weeks' worth of uppercuts, on many occasions he wasn't that scary, more of a bully than a teacher ever should be. Interestingly I did have a run in with the famous son of Tait later in life, many times, well before him and his gang were dismissed as rogue shit stains anyway.

Hanging around the local boozer, which was deep in enemy territory was common practice for me and Bob, it was important as a show of defiance.We would often brawl amongst the broken pint glasses in the carpark with the cheer of the pub drinkers looking on through dirty windows and smoke-stained curtains.We would often sneak into the bar for a glass of orange and stay there till the barmaid did her rounds and caught us trying to be older, "howay you two, you lot should know better" she would order us out under the boos and hisses of the lads.

Once after being ejected we passed a couple of fellas walking over to Frank and Chris looking shifty and nervous, keeping their distance "Frank, do you have trouble with big Woodsy?" one of them asks, I mean he had been sent to give Frank a message, so he must have known something. Me and Bob hung around to see what was going on, Chris jumped up, because that is what Chris did at the first sign of bother "what's the fucking score like?" he spoke for Frank on this occasion, "Woodsy wants a fight, down the yard" the messenger replied, he waited for a response which did not take long. Frank looked at Chris and smiled, "yea no problem" said Frank with ease and off they went.I heard every word and was worried, not that I could do anything but that was my bro. Later they were told that there was a unit cleared out in some scrapyardand Frank and Chris went on their own, not before a quick stop off at Chris's mothers. Frank picked out the biggest kitchen knife and wedged it in his trousers, "let's go Chris" and he grabbed a hammer on the way out.Some would have said this was madness this Woodsy bloke was bigger than Frank and Chris put together, he was about ninety foot but would that have stopped either of them?Not a chance they were afraid of no one.

Arriving at the yard there was a nice little crowd already there waiting, "I am not fucking arsed me kid", he whispered, Frank was a fearless bastard, but this was a serious mismatch but then by agreeing and turning up, Woodsy was rattled. Into the boot of his car, he reaches for a cricket bat, that looked like it had done a thousand runs.Now, this fight was uneven, Woodsy must have been weary, he was a giant, waving a bat in front of a five foot five unhinged madman who was happy to go that one step further, he just needed an opportunity to get close to himand it was game over. Frank goes in the hammer in one hand knife in the other, swinging the hammer then the knife, missing by inches.Woods swings the bat, clocks Frank on the head, Frank is dazed, he stumbles then gains his feet, Frank is then back in for round two, they clash Frankie's fast this time and they're split up, but the feeling was this was a set up from the start, tools placed in every corner of the yard, Chris and Frank had this all worked out, and laughed about it on the way there and so it was agreed that they were to go off alone somewhere else out of sight.

Everyone in the crowd waited, the air filled with silence and what was a lifetime that had passed, Chris was not in a good place right now, on edge fearing the worst, after what was seemingly hours the pair appeared, dispute settled, scuff marks on both faces, it's over, nobody had won or lost this one, but what was gained was respect.Both ways Frank had proven his point to never back down from an offer, this story echoed through the town, maybe with seasoning but this is how it happened.

Frank never liked to brag about his fights and troubles in front of us.I guess he never wanted us to emulate, or be proud of what he was doing, he knew his road was on a self-destructive pavement with unexpected bombs everywhere, we would always hear the stories second hand and I had my time with Woods myself later on in life by throwing him out of the club for misuse of narcotics, funny how things happen like that.

So me and Bob are, without realising it, running parallel lives with this lot, arranging to meet up with other people off other estates to have a square up, we would take turns me, then Bob, we were not arsed really, it was always the same result, some we would lose some we would win but we always laughed at the end, it was always important to laugh at the end, we would earn each other's respect, even today I am friends with many of my scuffles, so another quality in the tool bag that was very much needed for later in life.

So, it was the gym that kept us focused and my crazy pal Bob were smashing it.

Leaving school was easy, we never really felt like we were there if I am honest, school never taught us about life we had to find that out for ourselves, often the hard way. We were also heading for our very own holiday courtesy of the Queen, oh and a little help from that fucking Carta. Everything we did we did together, stole, fought, lied, even got locked up together, after pinching motorbikes and taking chases through the estate, led by the one and only Colin McCrae himself, he knew it was us just like he knew it was us on the scooter so after we lost him, because we always lost him, he just turned up at my house the next day, guns blazing like some crazy sheriff, pew pew. We ended up in court because that bike was connected to serious crime and Carta 'somehow' made it fit, that was his thing, he had a skill of making things happen, he was like a criminal tailor.In the cell before we were charged he would laugh, "fucking knew I would get you two, and that little stunt you both pulled off on the scooter, isn't going away either" he was referring to the robbery, but deep down he had fuck all, the only thing we got from that was a hundred and thirty two quid, and a few sleeves of fags, paid our gym for a while.

Nine months in a young offender gaff was not what we had planned but then who does, but it was time to use the tools that we had collected growing up, this shit was real, the gym meant we were bigger than the average and trouble was Bob's middle name remember, I was his back up and he was mine.

There were all sorts of villains in this place from different planets by the looks of it, I shared my plan with Bob, "Bob let's just keep our heads down, be nobodies and we're out in 3 month, there will be a gym here so we're laughing kid" "eh?" Bob replied, which was never a good sign, "if any daft cunt in here says a word to me al punch fuck out of every single one of them" his lips were tight, it was like he was visualising it, I could hear his knuckles cracking, so I guessed my plan was out the window, looks like we're punching fuck out every cunt then.

We're sat in that van, he was like a bull behind the gate. We learned a lot from the people we love the most, the scrap yard brawl taught us never to back down, loyalty and respect were pissing out of our pores, we were either gonna fit in here, or they would have to fit into us. We were brought onto the wing, it was like gladiators being pushed into the ring and what felt like millions of spotty bastards peering down, hanging over railings, pool games stopped, screws in plain clothes with bunches of keys tied to their hearts, "come on you two in ya go" whispered a friendly staff member, he was called big Ste, he looked after us, and we showed him the respect for that.

Surprisingly me and Bob weren't separated, which was perfect, we were shoved into a pad with two other lads from Newcastle.Now, these two weren't sure how to be with us, but we knew exactly how to be. "Areet, am Mack , and this is Bod" I guess he wanted to establish some rapport, rapport was Bob's job and he was good at it so I let him introduce us, "listen you pair of daft cunts, me and Dave want no shite from either of you, just so we are clear I will punch fuck out of the both of you, if you so much as breath near me right and if you so much as look at us al slap the fucking snot outtaya, I will fucking bounce you both off every fucking wall in this shithole" Bob is in the stance. I was a little more relaxed, these two idiots weren't giving us any bother.Bob managed to create an atmosphere that would scare a Honey Badger. "Areetareet man steady," Mack's plan didn't quite work out, he wanted to set the bar, but then again so did we and they accepted our way of thinking fairly rapidly.

Now, these two were just a couple of muppets, with shit posters on the wall that we're going to have to go, we knew there were bigger fish to get to and it either had to be done my way or Bob's way.At that, in pops a fat fucker who was clearly someone of interest, if we were to get a message through.He was much bigger than me and Bob but that never bothered us, the Frankie and Woods story sorted that one out. "I'm Podgy and if you two need anything you come see me yea" he said with a touch of intimidation, like what he was actually saying was, 'you will come to me.' Me and Bob both looked at each other and we laughed and said nothing but we were telepathically saying "do you want to do this or shall I bro." Podgy wasn't happy, "the fuck you laughing at?" He put himself in the stance which put Bob on full alert, so this one was mine.Stepping in was a must here, the pad wasn't big enough to take this bastard on, I needed to hurt him verbally which was a gift of mine, "look Porky, the only thing we need right now is for you to take your fucking fat self out of our pad, before I let my dog off its lead." Now Mack and Bod had lost their skin colour, they gave a fuck and we didn't, they developed a stutter in seconds, Podgy was having an impact on these two morons.Just as our new fat friend was about to open his trap, big Steve the friendly screw poked his head over his shoulder, "hew Podgy, watch ya self, these two are armed robbers" he winked at me, and then disappeared, leaving behind an uncertainty that Podgy couldn't process or take a risk with.We got the impression big Ste liked us, I guess we weren't like the spice smoking zombies that infested this place, we weren't about to walk about the wing like the undead, so we hung onto the armed robber title, I mean after all ironically it wasn't a lie.

So, there was a standoff with Podgy but it was a short lived one, because like the other two Geordies, he lost his colour and his fucking fat arse, he scurried off like a scared insect. We quickly made friends with our housemates, it made sense, they could be useful to us, they told us who was who and how things were in the place, which was interesting but we had no time for structure and hierarchy. Later that week, Podgy fancied his luck with Bob and me, he had been stalking us around the place like a small kitten that's not sure of how to pounce on the back of your heel, he must of been chewed up about our misunderstanding last week, we didn't hold any grudges if he kept his stupid looking face out our way we would all probably get along. He strolled over flanked by two of the jails finest ghosters, I mean these pale fucking day walkers weren't even looking the part but they had a role to play and you already know the rules about ghosting, it isn't fucking happening again.Bob suffered once and if Bob suffers, well you know how it works. "You two" murmured Podgy with a little more confidence I might add this time, this needed to be fast and hard we had discussed this was our plan, as he opened his fucking fat face to say whatever it was he wanted to say, both me and Bob let loose with a barrage, Podgy's wing man fell like a pensioner in the wind, so that left the man himself. Bob lands three shots, on target, he stumbles but catches Bob, the other wing man is on his toes and charging me down, we exchange blows and he's hurt, he lands a cracking shot on my temple, my hearing goes and I see stars, foolishly he gives me three or four seconds and that's all I need, so we're back at it trading like businessmen in Wall Street.Bob and Podgy are toe to toe, he's earning his money here, they both fall to the ground.The second wing man is back at me, I side step and spin this fucker like a roulette wheel, like a tag team I step in-betweenBob and Podgy as he shouts "come on ya fucking smoggy" beckoning us with both hands.Alarms and whistles are ringing, staff are running towards us, I need to finish this cunt before we are stopped, Bob steps in after his breather, right hook on an angle couldn't have landed it sweeter, Podgy is done the wing men are game over, staff everywhere me and Bob hands in the air, we are wrestled to the ground.Big Steve blows a whistle "back to your rooms now" he screams at the top of voice and everyone scatters like ants, the situation is well under control he strolls over to a wounded Podgy and whispers in his ear" I did warn you about these two didn't I?"

Off we go for a week down the block, carried in cuffs face down, I felt quite lonely down there and I guess Bob did too.Me and the big man were rarely apart, it was time to reflect, think about the outside and what we wanted, it was dark and quiet, even though Bob was ten feet away in another cell, he may as well of been in another country. Things were different when we came out of there we were taller and had gained an invisible stone and a half.We walked around the place like Teessider's on a dust fuelled Saturday night, we weren't arsed about who did what on the landing, all we wanted everyone to know was that we weren't to be fucked about with.Bob would have gone again in an instant, but we really didn't need to, the others all seemed to have a quiet understanding and an appreciation for what we did.Podgy can do what he wants, we took a piece of him last week, a piece he can't get back, a piece that now belongs to us and that made us laugh.We did spend a little more time in that place than we had wanted but it was worth it in the end. We left Podgy behind and am quite sure he would have picked up where he left off when our cell door was closed and Mack and Bod turned out to be sound lads who we kept in touch with.We would send them a postal order now and then with the odd letter talking shit about how the world was and he would keep us informed of the stories that Podgy adds a little 'seasoning' to.

Shitbag's and slinks...

The term 'Shitbag' is not an attack on the capability of an individual, some of the biggest shitbags in Teesside of yesteryear and today are very capable and can handle themselves well, some of the toughest people in this shit hole are indeed shitbags because of how they conduct their business, it's more of a description of their personality or character and in spite of things being different now from back in them days, one thing that has remained pretty much the same throughout time is the deceit and blatant disregard for the very things we were spoon fed like respect, loyalty and trust, it became our badge, our coat of arms.

Amongst the streets and in the cracks in the houses that were held together by lies and blue giro's, were the fake smiles and handshakes that were as translucent as a glass window pane.A pat on the back and the wink from that bloke you know that may as well wear a uniform, or maybe they are already wearing one plain clothes, the place is littered with people doing deals with people they drink with and don't trust, the law has it sewn up and turning people on each other is easy for them, allowing kings to rule on their say so and terms. Not us, we have standards these fuckers can't reach, high on the top shelf, our lot can't be puppets it's not in the blood and there isn't a price on how we live our lives.When you're educated in the real world by people who write the scripts, you can't be like the rest. It took time to work through the estates, who can we trust and who to swerve, who we need to return the pretend smile to and to find this out we needed to take risks, but we had a system handed down like that old pair of Nike. We made good money and kept our gym membership for the year, growing was still the priority and keeping fit was essential but this town had, and still has, a habit of offering soldiers to the other side like a sacrificial lamb, in some dirty trade in a pub somewhere out of the way, for every ten that got through, one failed and it would be under circumstances that had a bit of a smell.

Having a ride out into the country was a common thing for me n Bob.Frank and Chris would often send us into a village post office to buy a stamp or two, report on the staff and the goings on, only for the fucking place to be robbed two weeks later.

Bob's eternal flame would ignite at the sight of a post office that was always odd, his desire to empty one was never right. Now and then it was funny, or maybe not, to see an undercover police car parked next to a 'familiar' number plate in the car park of that country boozer out the way, disgusting to say the least but this is Teesside and that's how these folks hold onto their crowns, I guess their freedom was and is as precarious as the soul they were about hand over, but their sociopathic personalities took care of any emotional connection with the victim. What we knew was that we had done a few bits of work for this bloke and Bob reminded me that we had a little job to do for him, this was something we had to think about it was to be our last, mistrust started to taste like milk that was sour and after what we have seen in the pub car park this milk needed pouring down the sink.

We usually waited at the phone box for a call but we figured that we needed to change things around this time, no calls in specific filthy phone boxes out in the open, we just called to his home on a scooter, kept our helmets on and arranged to call by at the time agreed, this was different for him interestingly he asked why we weren't at the phone box, didn't matter this was a gamble and we were not about to be handed over to his blue pals. Our plan was simple we talked it through with Frank, he did not want it to go ahead but thought our plan was brilliant, "you're fucking mad you two, but if you pull this off I will buy you a drink" he laughed but I knew he was nervous on our behalf. Chris, on the other hand, wanted us to go right ahead like a fucking train off the tracks "it will work, Frank leave them alone" he whispered to our kid with full confidence. That afternoon me and Bob went to town with a couple of borrowed ten pound notes offChris. He was funding this shit because he knew why this had to happen, our aim was to buy two small gym bags identically the same, first part out the way. We spent the next few hours talking and even rehearsing the next bit, pen and paper, then out on the scooter then back, the job was that we just had to drop off a package, seemed a simple one.

I remember switching bags swiftly with Bob at some point and then getting pulled over by a marked police car almost straight away, after running a search on my name, cars pulled in from everywhere, it was like they came from the sky. The unmarked drug squad, it was like the fucking

Sweeney n all tha "what's in the bag?" I was confident because Bob had the goods in the other bag, "just a loaf of fucking bread what the fuck is this?" I shouted as I was slammed against the bonnet of the car, American style and cuffed like I was a fucking murderer, it was no surprise to me to see the old bill stood scratching their heads and muttering to themselves, as they turn the bag inside out like a favourite crisp packet to lick it clean, only to find a mothers pride thick slice.Of course, the plod were more confused than our man was later when I told him they let me go but took the bag, he couldn't say a word, after all, it was his set up, the cunt tried to hand me and Bob over as gift to the Babylon, now we were fuming but could do fuck all but keep the real package as a payment for his treachery, needless to say we never bothered with this cunt ever again and to this day he is still on the radar, one to watch or swerve, I think deep down he often wonders what really happened that day but then his boys in blue would have told him the bag was empty, or was it? That was up to them to wonder, or argue between themselves.

We made a tidy sum that day and Frank, Norman and Chris laughed for months, they moved the package elsewhere you see they had the means and the trust in people, but they gained knowledge into a cunt they once did business with.You see this is the jungle we live in with snakes in the grass and looking over your back was just a way of life. These gangsters couldn't handle life on the inside of the big fence, which gave the law an advantage that they abused, we let you live you keep us right, Bob and Dave were not fucking gifts on this occasion, or on any occasion, no one ghosts us. We were brought up around watching your back and each other's something that failed one night with Chris and Frank, he was betrayed and let down beyond words, by the very people he sat and laughed with, people he would have called friends lured him out of the local one night, whilst sat amongst faces, into a car for a journey that was to lead him to a nightmare. Chris walks into the pub looking for Frank and spots blood all over the toilet wall, "what the fuck is that, in the toiletswhose blood is that?" Chris asks, part of him is worried he knows because Frankie is nowhere to be seen, everybody looks at each other with none of them quite know what to say, "its Frankie Taylors Chris" one of them says, "are you fucking kidding me, what the fuck?" shouts Chris he's going crazy, "what the fuck happened where is he?" he is hysterical, "he's gone off in a car Chris, what could we do" Chris is fuming, his pal could be anywhere, but he had a bad feeling about the whole thing.

Meanwhile, Frank was taken to a pub, in a rough part of town, the route to the pub told him everything, he knew where he was going and he knew what this was all about, he got out of the car and had plenty of opportunity to bail, he wasn't afraid of what was about to happen this cunt could not take Franks soul or his heart, I mean my brother could run but this is Frank we're talking about, the man has more pride than the whole pub could imagine, he has more bottle than the dairy, he walks in and the door closes flanked by two blokes, standing at the bar, was that bloke from inside, Duffy, unfortunately, he hadn't forgotten about Frankie and his lack of commitment to support him taking over the Makems, Frank knew this, and so Duffy attacked Frank right there in the pub. Frank took everything he gave him, he did leave him in a state he had never been in before, his face was smashed and twice the size, see this is how a bully works. Eventually, Frank was taken to the hospital he was physically in a bad way and mentally he had one thing on his mind, you can't beat people that have a big heart, you just can't beat people like Frankie Taylor, a mean you have kill cunts like him. Chris was devastated, me and Bob were not allowed up the hospital, he got word to us that he was ok and that was enough. I spoke to him on the phone and the first thing he said was "he never knocked me out kid, he couldn't do it." I was just upset that my brother was lying in hospital, Chris was by his bedside and something had changed here, "I am going to get him mate" Frank muttered under his broken jaw "have you still got that thing?" He asked."Of course mate." Frank was referring to the shotgun me and Bob used on that van. Chris broke down he was gutted, this should not have happened, friends had lured him out of that pub, slinks had stepped aside and watched him climb into that motor, he knew who they were and so do we, to this very day we know what happened. Teesside was a bad place with people selling their souls like cowards, we know who you are.

Frank recovered and stayed focused on what he wanted to do, this little cunt was unhinged.Sometime later Frank had word that Duffy was out and about, drinking in town.The time was right and the rage that filled him when he was laid in the hospital bed was just a strong now as it was then. "Where you going kid?" I asked nervously. I knew something was up, I could tell by his face, he was on the phone and he wouldn't tell me who to, he normally would tell us everything but this was different. I was worried sick he was acting strange, he looked at me and Bob and one corner of his mouth made a half-hearted smile, "be good," he said with a tone that felt like he meant it, he ruffled my hair and his eyes spoke, I felt like I wasn't going to see him again, "can we come with you?" I replied, I just had a bad feeling, "no, I will be sound kid, stay cool", he often said "stay cool" but I always felt like I wouldn't see him again in these moments. He left the house, a car crept into the street like it was tip toeing, I thought I saw my older brother Norman sat in the back and this would always mean serious shit.The lights were turned off and the car held its breath like it didn't want to disturb the neighbours. I couldn't see who was driving but Frank climbed onto the back seat, it was late early hours.

Me and Bob were left guessing and we came up with all sorts of shit, the whole thing didn't sit right, Frank, Norm and two others in the middle of the night, no this was fucked up. Frank had driven to a part of the town and parked up near our Gym, it was 03:30 in the morning, he had word that Duffy was at a party on the outskirts of the town centre, they sat in silence for a short while, all of them were taking a huge risk just being there, from nowhere out popped two barrels as cold as ever, she wants to breathe again, Frank popped a couple of cartridges in the old girl to wake her up, all you could hear was the cozy fit as they slid into place, he really was going to do this, his face was serious, his eyes had glossed over, without evena hood or a mask he wanted this fucker to see his face, he wanted his face to be the last he saw, he had already done a deal with the devil, he was ready.

The clock ticked and they continued to wait, as calm as ever nobody spoke a word. Frank was slow breathing to steady his heart rate, then suddenly there is a spill onto the road, bodies everywhere, there is trouble and lots of noise up ahead, shouting, screams and a fight breaks out with two men, Frank opens the door, "Frank wait, it's him he's fighting with someone, wait kid," Frank has one foot out of the door 20 meters away, both hands clasping the shooter till his knuckles turned white, the fight continues then there is screaming, one man falls to the floor struggling, "it looks like he's game over Frank" whispers the driver, Frank opens the door again, "no Frank wait, it looks bad." Frank steps out of the car and walks towards the scuffle, he fights to keep two barrels jammed under his arm, he stops yards away from a lifeless man, he walks backwards to the car, as the blue lights are seen in the background, sirens everywhere, screams and people turning a blind eye walking away like they seen nothing, "Frank we best get out of here, get that put away."

This was Frank's opportunity, he needed to be sure, the man on the floor is still. Frank smiles to himself, fuck knows what was going through his mind at that point.He unloads the shotgun, looks at the cartridges and lets out a puff of air, tucks them away safely and as they pull off the kerb there is no movement from the man on the floor.Passers-by whispering amongst themselves, "Duffy is a goner" his last fight and tonight it was always going to be his last, it just so happened someone got there first. This was a gift for Frank, he smiled and sits back in the car takes a deep breath wondering if Duffy had noticed him standing close by, "fucking yes" he shouts, "the Lord works in mysterious ways hey kid" he punches the air and part of him had been restored in that moment. Frank always fantasised after this that his face was the last, he was prepared to go away and knew that it could have been likely. "Who wants a fucking drink" he taps the driver on the shoulder "let's go kid."He partied hard that week and celebrated, it may seem a little macabre but he had his reasons and he never forgot the people that turned their backs on him, they are not protected anymore and now I guess the same people will never forget what they did either, Frankie was a friend you would never want to lose, but once you did well, you did.

On we grow...

It was still the plan to get big, have money and slap any daft cunt that got in the way. That was always the mission.We had plenty of membership in the gym and if that ran out Mick was always good to me and Boband if he wasn't good to us Bob would just threaten to take the fucking gym off him anyway.Steel City was our home and big Mick knew that if we were in there worshiping the steel, then we were not getting ourselves into bother, he was like our guardian and we repaid him by keeping the place right when he wasn't there, having a word with the younger members if they were abusing the equipment. This was good discipline and Bob always loved having a word, "eh you what?" Beating personal bests and copying the juiced up legends in there was always a laugh, these fucking monsters could lift a bus and eat a cow straight after, but could they do twenty five rounds? Could they fuck, we were always taught to keep a good balance of both, keep strong and fit was the message from a bloke we met in there Micky The Sarge.Now the sarge was only five ten, with a flat top and the soul of a stallion, we called him The Sarge because he was like a military man, he was a machine, he didn't have veins and blood, it was more like cables and oil, a doorman from the town with skills, he would bash us up a bit in the bag room cost us a few ribs but it was all good stuff, he seen real potential in Bob and me and after a while and an increase in weight, he asked us if we wanted to work with him and a few other lads, we weren't sure, well I wasn't but Bob was like "yea well aye, count us in Mick we'll do it."Bob steamed in guns blazing without asking what the fucking work was.Mick laughed a lot at Bob, not in a bad way, I think he knew the cunt was not wired up right, then again Mick was like a soldier on the beach at Dunkirk, this bloke was like a cocked loaded gun ready at all times.

So, the work, well a couple of kids our age owed Mick a few quid and mick didn't really have the time to chase it up.He gave us the address and the amount owed, "lads fifty percent, you get it I will half it with ya." Mick laughed, but we see this as an opportunity, "let's go straight from the gym Dave, I have a bat in the shed." "Sound," I gathered some tools and we went up to the address, it was a flat with an intercom, we buzzed up, nothing, then two lads coming out of the flat stairwell made eye contact. "What you after lads?" One of the scruffy bastards asked, with a spliff bigger than his arm poking out of his mouth, "what do they call you fuck face?" Bob asked, he cautiously told us his name which matched with the name on our bit of paper, it was a bit like a movie scene, were at this point we pull out a pistol with a silencer on it, double tap him then leave, only it wasn't. "Now then, have you heard of Bob and Dave?" I quizzed him and he looked confused. "Nah never heard of either of them" at that Bob smashes the pair of them all over the stairs, a mean upper cutting these bastards for a week, "argh, fucking hell man get off us" they both screamed like little girls, "you never heard of Bob and Dave?" I repeated,this time I was crouched in front of them, "no, no have a fuck" he whimpered. "Well you fucking have now!" His swollen face tried to open an eye, like a newborn wanting to see his Mother, we were anything but this cunts Mother. "What do you want, eh what the fuck do you want?" He cried, "Micky, you owe Micky six hundred quid yea?" I slapped him on the head "argh, get off fuck sake" he pleaded and he was in pain, feeling sorry for himself, his mate never moved. "I have it here I was goanna ring him a swear." This sounded like a lie so I slapped him again, he reached into his pocketand amongst, money bags of weed, pills, and loose tobacco that has escaped from the lose fags he carries, was Mick's money. I slapped his head again and I swear I could hear his brain rattle. I took the money and it was exactly there, maybe he was going to ring Mick, well it's done now. "Now don't let me or Bob have to come back here again ok?" They both remained in the foetal position until we had disappeared.Mick had been looking for this little shitbag for weeks and we bump into him in five minutes, we hand The Sarge his six hundred over and he was surprised "Did you get it? Fuck me no way" he laughed out loud and told us he had wrote that money off, we told him the story as it happened, adding seasoning was something Bob and me never needed to do.So Mick split the money three ways, this was a bonus "fucking hell nice oneMick" Bob shouted folding his money up and stuffing it down his sock. Bob always kept his money there, in case he got robbed, the irony eh, maybe a lesson from this would be to ask for the money first, before splattering folk all over the place, the cunt would of handed it over, we chortled about that for a while often wonder if the lad would of got Bob's wrath anyway, he hated a cheeky cunt and The Sarge was someone we respected.

Nights out become easy, doormen would let our underage arses in bars, on The Sarges say so, a quick nod from him and we were safe, this was a great perk.We never took the piss and always asked permission to smash some fucker in the bogs, "make it quick" The Sarge would tell us straightening his coat and turning a blind one.It was always quick and never a brawl, taxing bags of dust was easy, then The Sarge and his team would come in and hoover up any mess.Sometimes the job would be for the doorman, we would get the nod and maybe a description, job done, we were like a two man wrecking crew you cheek The Sarge or you give the doorman shit on your way in, the twins (me and Bob) would mark your cards or your head.

It was always going to happen, bumping into familiar enemies from school, the likes of Smigga and his lot, fuck me we hadn't seen this little rat in years, I mean we had heard shit about him, this shit stain had a girlfriend and a baby, the scumbag circle of life starts again. He was never alone and always had three or four with him, just like the old days, "Bob, remember that cunt?" I nudged Bob elbowing his ribs. I think I wanted to irritate him before he made eye contact with Smigga, like poking a dog through a cage, I laughed under my breath "remember that little shite hawk who ghosted you he proper dropped you didn't he? "Now I was laughing out loud, I was having fun here watching my pal turn red."Yes I fucking do!" Bob wasn't laughing, which made it even more hilarious, I boxed The Sarge off, who got on the radio and blind eyed all his team for the quickest showdown on the dance floor one night, Smigga and his three shit bag pals who were selling dust, yes they were, we knew this and passed that onto The Sarge.

Me and Bob knew we had two a piece, The Sarge laughed, "now this I got to see" his money was on us but the team weren't that hopeful. "Come on Bob let's get this shit over with I need a drink" I shouted over the loud music., Bob was always ready we know this, all four were on the dance floor being a nuisance.We made our way through the crowd crouched down, like we were swimming with the salmon, we popped up in front of them like a couple of Jack in the box, it took them a couple of seconds to realise who we were and it was when they all took their eyes off us and looked at each other like lost sheep, we were transported back to the playground, rats looking for orders, looking for their way out, the strobe light making this all look like the opening scene out of the movie 'Blade', doorman counting to ten before stepping in.We had to be fast, it was two a piece, my first fell like a domino, Bob throws two shots first one missed, he blamed the lighting, that left hook The Sarge had been working on came up trumps, two shitbags down time to trade, my second wanted to dance, I kept it tight all three shots landed but he was still alive, we exchanged blows but this cunt has nothing then I connect with two of my finest and he takes a seat, Bob had put Smigga to kip hours ago and was laughing at me from the side with The Sarge.In come the clear up team with their own style of cleaning up, bear in mind this only took a total of ten seconds, I thought we did ok. "Fuck me Dave I thought I was gonna have to bail you out there." Bob and The Sarge shared the same joke that I was part of but was never allowed in on.

We often stayed back for the odd drink with the lads and they would poke fun at our shit shirts and hair gel, "ere Mick give them a white shirt, fucking naughty these two," big Andy bellowed from behind the bar, he laughed and then paused, that started out as a joke but left The Sarge thinking, "what do you think Dave?" Sarge whispered and Bob was like a school kid that knew the answer and wanted to put his hand up, he turned to Bob "what about you fella?"" Am in if he's in" we gave each other the nod as keen as mustard, "leave it with me, al see what a can do."

In them days you didn't need a licence, or to be trained, you just had to be game as fuck. Sarge gave us a wink and then we would bum a lift to wherever we were going, I guess we had been doing a real life job interview over the last few months, The Sarges team was tight and all of them were up for war, Bob and me were amongst the smallest but together we were double the trouble, our communication was on point if Bob throws a shot I would follow up with two more, without even asking, it was like a dance.

Weekends were brilliant Thursday, Friday and Saturday we would iron our white shirts crisp, almost filling the sleeves and with a black clip on tie, checking each other over in the mirror, hair gel on point and polished doc martens, we supplied our own aftershave now, several bottlesand even shared with Frank which was refreshing. Frank was working shifts in a different part of town with Norman and my other brother Marty. Marty was a laugh and also a handful, a ladies man he was in the game for the smash but could be right at your side before you even asked him. It wasn't long before we were getting offers to work other places.We earned nicknames 'live and wire' which followed us around from club to club, we were often used as the first in, bash up the place then a heavy team would step in and do the lifting, it worked well, it wasn't uncommon to hear over the radio "dance floor, dance floor live wire" that was mine and Bob's instructions and we knew what we had to do, arrive, bash every cunt in sight that looked like they were involved, even bash any cunt that wasn't then back off for a clean-up, usually took thirty seconds tops.There was no style or panache to how we got things done, we just did, and this was our world.

After a short time we learned how to make money and keep ourselves sharp over the whole weekend.Weekdays we trained, weekends we were gladiators, we bashed people from Northumberland right down to York and across Cumbria. The name live and wire had reached places, idiots had come from Newcastleand from Carlisle to see what they could do with us, we punched fuck out of everybody, working inside was where we were suited.

A coach arrived from Carlisle, we knew this bunch were up for it, "have a good night lads, no bother yea" warned our head guy but me n Bob knew there was a bunch of lads at the back curious about us two, pointing, whispering, "alright" a sarcastic Bob muttered "aye sound" replied the bunch, they were chewy in the queue so what were they going to be like with a few lines of dust in their empty shells. "Take a radio Boband go inside keep an eye on that lot, any shit off them shout for the lads, you know the crack." The boss was thinking what we were and my sleeves got rolled up. Bob looked at me and laughed "fuck sake Dave, if your sleeves are getting rolled, we must be in for a night." I slapped his back and joined in the laugh, "let's go pal", the other lads would laugh when they saw me and Bob and our enthusiasm for our work.We worked with a few old school chaps, these fellas can rumble but they would rather not if that makes sense, it was all about the easy shift for these guys.

Inside was a different place it was dark, loud and it was us against them, the potential being everyone and anyone in there, which does not sound fair, but Bob and me liked the unpredictability of the numbers, it gave us a buzz, but tonight we knew who the drama crew were, the Carlisle lot who took an interest in us. With sleeves rolled up and our radio volume on number eight we scoped the club side by side like a couple of squaddies on the drill square, alert looking left and right, with narrow eyes focusing on quick hands and people doing prolonged handshakes near the bogs.We timed how long it took to do a full circle back to where we started so we knew exactly where the Carlisle lot were.There were six of them in this mob and there was a leader, with at least four others that needed not to be underestimated.Minimum eye contact was made, there was no need to wind these fuckers up, they were already in that place, but I guess Bob was being Bob, that always lead us to bother, we were the only lads that always brought a spare shirt to work. Towards the end of the night, which was fairly settled really with only a handful of incidents to manage, on one of our patrols we edged nearer the Carlisle lot and our path was blocked!It didn't feel right or safe so we took it up a notch, three of them had their tops off, half decent nick I would say but this wasn't allowed, I calmly gestured for them to put their tops back on, one did straight away the other two kept jumping up and down like some sort of tribal African war dance, I mean who knows what goes on in Carlisle?!So Bob leans forward, it's ready to go here "do us a favour lads put your tops back on" he insisted, whilst this was happening, I was on the radio "front door are you there, might need a clean-up team at bar two, clean up at bar two," a pre-emptive strike felt necessary here but we gave it one more shot. The leader was a classic leader, we had already discussed that if he fell his team would fall.From two different directions I could see the cavalry making their way through the crowd, the leader was our focus he had a lot to say in the queue, I figured he knew about us strangely.Two clean up teams yards away had noticed me and Bob in the centre of a hurricane with half a dozen out of town wannabe's.Just then the leader leans forward and shouts "I have been sent to test you" I heard what he said, but I pretended I didn't and asked him to repeat himself and so he did, well he attempted to, "I have been sent here to..," was as far as he got, I bashed his knee on the inside with a leg strike, this idiots night was actually over, Bob let two go sharp, I followed with a lightning three shots all landing, it was in full swing, the clean-up team had set off they were moments away, the strobes and loud music still drown the action. Bob and me were making a mess of this crew, even though we shed some of our own claret and lost buttons, in come the cleaners and we back off fresh hands on, game over for this lot, we needed to know what the test was all about, because from where we stood that was no test, he fell first like a domino, but who had sent him was the question, who had sent this bastard to test live and wire?

Later we learned that this bunch of halfwits were doormen that worked a club Cumbria, their boss was some shit bag that had dealings with shit bags in Teesside, so what the fuck did that have to do with us, maybe we taxed someone and it hit his pocket or we hurt someone close to him, who knows but Bob wanted to square this cunt away, he had sent a test now where is the real thing?

WHY DRIVE WHEN YOU CAN JUST FLY, I WILL JUST SIT HERE. ALL BACK OF THE BUS."

DAVE

6

Double Barrel Mayhem

Our crazy weeks and days turned into a blur we bashed trouble causers on a weekly basis.Things hadn't changed at all with me and Bob, we lived by the same rules and values and that kept us right, we would find ourselves in fights with naughty people who just wanted a pop at Bob or Dave or us both.

We ran into a big second hand car dealer from Leeds who had heard rumours of two vicious little dogs from Teesside, he spent a lot time around this shit hole and visited our place for a drink one night.He arrived relaxed and curious at the same time, dropping hints about hearing stories of our exploits.He looked like a large version of Freddie star, he was repeating the tales with a hint of sarcasm, probably to size us up, we met briefly in the door way and he tapped Bob on the head like he was a little boy, well that went down like a fart in a lift "whoa whoa steady on big man" I whispered as I stopped his hand from starting a war I don't think he was ready for.Bob turned sharply "the fuck are you?Al punch your fucking head in yadivvi," snapped Bob. "Steady lads" he nervously replied and pulled his hand back real quick like a dog had just went for him, both me and Bob are now like dancing partners in the stance, "I can see why you two are called live wire" strange that he knew our names.This was another one of them situations, we figured he had come to take a trophy back to Leeds.

This was becoming all too familiar, people from out of town popping through to see us uninvited, he chuckled to himself but we never really found it funny, we had to keep an eye on this fucker all night, he wanted something, we weren't sure what,I mean he wasn't drinking and he was dressed a little too casual for my liking.

Later that night after leaving the club for home, I noticed there was a Range Rover parked with two hefty silhouettes, right beside our ride home. Bob was on red alert, we were always on alert in this no man's land between leaving the club and getting home.We unlocked the car, then we both stretched off.Out pops Mr grown up from Leeds, nice and steady "lads look, about earlier I just want to say it was a bit of misunderstanding yea" he muttered with his palms showing, but he was getting closer, he was walking towards us, he didn't need to get close he could have said this from a comfortable distance and fucked off, one more step and I knew Bob was going for him, we always threw the first shot that was our thing, he reached into his pocket, could have been going for a fucking comb, but that was Bob's cue, he landed the first shot crisp, sounded like a fire cracker, then traded like a true salesman, shot for shot, both fell against the shutter but Bob held onto this big cunt. Bob was doing ok, then the passenger jumped out, this was always the plan, "fucking back off" I held my hand out keeping him away, he steps forward in his little vest only to be bashed, three or four shots landing, his arms were big but he was stiff, he threw me against the same shutter and came in like he had already won but that left hook of mine was given to me by The Sarge and I used it, well game over. Bob was still doing ok, he throws this bastard on the ground two kicks to the head, the passenger didn't like what he was seeing, he picked himself up off the floor, I guess he was meant to take Bob or me fast, but it didn't quite work out that way, he wanted to rescue his pal I think that was their plan, "you alright Joff" he shouts in a worried tone. Bob let him back up "come on come on ya big cunt" Bob screamed and is bouncing up and down, he beckoned him forward with both hands, they clashed more trades. Bob was accurate and technically on point, he is in charge here, this went on for about seven minutes, Bob head butts this lump then followed up with the sharpest right, left hook then it was all over, Mr grown up fell against the shutter, his pal edging forward face covered in the red stuff, he staggered. Bob was on his toes "come on you fat cunt" Bob screamed, he wasn't ready for a rumble, his pride was in tatters, the passenger rescued him pushes him into the car, I am checking Bob over, there was claret, bit off Bob and a bit off Mr grown up, they reversed back and Mr grown up gave us a two fingered salute, not sure if this was respect or a simple goodbye. "Fuck me he was strong" said Bob "who the fuck was that?" After they left we roared out laughing "nightmare that, new fucking shirt this" Bob moaned, he always moaned about torn shirts.I think the local shirt shop must of thought we were nuts. We carried on laughing, to later find out off Frank that was Joffa, bit of a name round Leeds and Teesside. Frank had some bother in jail with him and Chris wanted to cut him up over some gear or something.Well, he felt a bit of Bob tonight and as usual we moved on from it like it never happened.

We pondered over the Carlisle lot, we weren't happy about it one bit, wondering who the fuck had sent someone to test Bob and me and why? We wanted to pop and see this cunt in person, seriously we wanted to take his shit to his doorstep, "it's the only way" Bob shrugs, "I think so too bro." It didn't take long to find out who was who in their neck of the woods, that shithole only had a handful of bars and a couple of clubs so we guessed these idiots were easy to find.

Bob wanted to drive through and just take them on right before their shift started, our homework told us it was a small club with three on the front door, and four inside we knew we could take three no problem and we wanted a bit of an audience.There is nothing like having a reputation dismantled in front of the ordinary people.So we drive across to this dump, through a few villages and spotted some potential graft along the way, "Bob, let's just do thisand get back to Boro tonight" I tapped him on the chest " you fucking hear me numbnuts?" Bob lets out a dry cough "yea mate" I wasn't sure how to take that but that was the plan.

Once we were there we clocked the front door, we had a little look around see which way we would be heading after, seems straight forward enough.Opening time there is a bit of a queue, a line full of scruffy bastards all inbred, so I join the line keeping my head down, shuffling forward, saying nothing, So I am near the front door and Bob better fucking hurry up, then Bob strolls over tracksuit bottoms, gym boots and a black Slazenger vest looking sharp, just in front of me is the idiot from our club who was sent to test us and the boss who we figured was calling the shots.It's all tense, they noticed Bob but didn't recognise him, the boss steps forward and is right in front of me, my head is down and he has his arm up against my chest to stop the flow of human traffic, his boys step to Bob "not tonight marra" one of them says and laughs under his breath. Bob looks up "you not remember me pal?" Bob smiles and the doorman is trying to figure out who the fuck this cunt is, he frowns as his tiny brain searches his memory, then like a lightbulb moment his eyes widen, he makes eye contact with the boss and tilts his head towards Bob.This whole process is taking seconds but it's all in slow motion, what they don't know is it's all game over before we start and all way too late for these farmers to do a single fucking thing about it.The penny drops with the boss, he realises something is wrong, but can't make the connection, he turns to me "just hold it there mate will ya" at that moment the idiot who is dealing with Bob clocks me in the queue, then puts it all together like some jigsaw puzzle, but it's too late, like synchronized swimmers in an Olympic competition, I let go on the boss, I connect like a plug in the wall and he falls straight on his arse hands still in his long Crombie pockets, whilst Bob is dancing with two each one left right, next one left right, the boss shakes his head, on his way up I hit him with a barrage of shots claret spoils his front of house, "we have come to test you, fucking shit bags, remember us now big man?" I shouted in front of all his locals, the whole line of punters see the whole thing, me and Bob are now dancing on our toes, we finished the other two doormen fast and knew we had to nash, side by side the boss didn't want to know, we left him wiping the red stuff from his face and with his reputation around Carlisle slowly draining down the gutter with the drizzle of rain, as the locals all watched on preparing their version of the whole event to spread around the place, whatever reputation they had, me and Bob just changed all that, this was our aim, humiliate.

He backed off looking defeated, picking his staff up off the floor whilst calling for the police and more re-enforcements. "Time to go kid" Bob tapped me on the arm, we were off, job was done.We legged it round the block full pelt to the car like a couple of athletes, we needed to get out of here, opening the car we heard footsteps behind us, several sets, getting louder, "down here lads" one shouts out of breath, these fuckers are after doing us in, as I turn Bob is under the passenger seat like he's lost his wallet "Bob fuck you doing hurry up" I shouted in a whisper, I am ready to go again hands up, this time it would have been a struggle, four maybe five fresh sets of hands onto me and Bob what were our chances. Bob has other plans and out the corner of my eye I see him standing there with two barrels at the waist all the doormen halt in their tracks like they have come to the end of a cliff edge, they all turned a shade of grey that not even dulux can produce "fucking back off" shouts Bob, we're in charge here and all hands are up walking backwards like it was an old fashioned stick up. "Start the car"Bob calmly whispers.These doormen aren't going anywhere but the toilet to check their pants. Bob climbs in with two barrels still trained on these vulnerable cowards who clearly thought a good kicking in the ally was fitting for two cheeky cunts from Teesside.The door slams, we are off, in the rear view I see one of them throwing up, I needed to have a word with Bob but once we were clear of this shithole, "Bob what the fuck are doing bringing that?" I shook my head because all I could see was prison.Bob laughed and rubbed my shoulders like it was gonna relax me, "Dave, I never brought any cartridges man relax," he laughed, just like my brother Frankie and he didn't give a fuck either.

I knew things would heat up when we got back home so I cleaned everything up and we went about our business.Three days later we got a visit from the blue boys, they were subtle but to the point, asked about our whereabouts on that night, "I was at home with my brother, go and ask him" I quickly muttered, "your fucking brother eh, how convenient." I knew Frank would switch himself on and verify anything I had said, these fellas aren't stupid, but then neither were we.A big copper we haven't seen before leans into us and whispers "look lads you keep out of trouble and we will all get along, you won't ever see us, but if that little stunt had anything to do with you two fucking idiots, I will have you ok?" Bob pipes up instantly "what stunt, fuck you talking about?" this was met with "shhhhh" he taps the side of his nose, "I will see you later boys" and they leave. "Fuck sake they know" I was worried, as usual Bob laughed it off, "if they knew we'd be locked up kid." It wasn't very reassuring but there was something soothing about what Bob just said that made sense.

Stay cool...

Over time we had met some unsavoury people and made useful connections, this always lead us to be constantly looking over our shoulders but this is how we were brought up and we only ever really trusted our own.

We had offers of work that carried risks and had a decent wage attached to it but we often said no because of who was involved.If our Frank asked us or the work was endorsed by him we would sign up immediately.So when me and Bob were asked about a job out of town with the people we trust the most it was a no brainer really.All our work was out of town, we couldn't trust many folk in this place and this was a job Bob had been waiting for pretty much all his life thinking about his younger days. This was risky but trust was never in question when it comes to the outcome, and we enjoyed working with this lot, we were old enough now and we could hold our own. We had been talking about a large cash job for some time. I had friends who used to work for a security firm and gave us information about how their systems worked, it was foolproof, on paper it was easy money, it would be late at night, no one would get hurt, guards are trained to just hand it over, it's only money and it wasn't theirs, the briefcases had sensors which exploded red dye all over the cash when stolen, Frank and Chris couldn't get their heads around this bit, they saw this as a problem, we never.

We had to let the heat fade away from me and Bob, Frank would laugh about us at times and joke, "am not going anywhere with you two your bang on top" then Chris would join in "ere I heard you two are pinned on the wall in doggy nick" "ere fuck off man we have done nowt for ages" I said trying to convince myself that me and Bob were going straight, Bob drinking a can of coke spat the lot out as he remembered something from only the other night, "see, that cunt gives it away all the time" Frank laughed. "What do you think Chris?" Frank asks with a more serious tone, Chris was Chris, did he need asking really, "ok we will leave it for a couple of weeks.

Time had passed and I spoke to my man on the inside, he gave us times and places.The plan was to hit the guards as they refill one of three cash machines, fast.We decided to hit the post office, it was out of the way with good roads on the way out, the money boxes have a device that was connected to receivers on the guards belt, now when the box and the belt are separated more than twenty meters the box would explode, dyeing all the cash red, and this would be a problem, no fucker would know this except the guards and they would happily hand the case over with a smile, thinking the money would be no goodbut I had other plans. All the drops were done at night this was a fast hit, two mins tops, we waited.You could almost hear heartbeats in the car, you could hear Bobs brain thinking out loud, the air freshener was replaced with the smell of adrenaline, everyone had a job to do and if we all do our jobs we're laughing. Bob has two barrels, so does Chris, we don't need anything else, I was to orchestrate the whole thing. I had a range of accents I could use, it might sound daft but if the law were looking for a gang of cockneys or jocks it might just be enough to throw them off. We take up positions the clock begins, the van arrives on time and out pops the passenger, he bangs on the side of the van twice and the big silver draw spits out two cases, the guard is whistling his favourite song by Sinatra with not a care in the world, this is just another nights work for him, he turns and is startled "argh fuck" he yells silently, 25 seconds past. Old two barrels widens her nostrils and is now staring right at him like he bullied her in school and she isn'tgonnablink.He's standing there with our cases like a lost Dad at the airport glaring at the departure board, only this guy has just seen a ghost, out of nowhere steps Chris, face covered with only his eyes glued open, now it's my turn 40 seconds in. "Stand still, and stay cool we haven't come here for you, we have come for our money, it doesn't belong to you, do you understand?" I bellowed like a Sergeant major on the drill square.After a slight pause the guard did what he was trained to do and handed the cases to Frank like there was a mix-up on the carousel at Leeds Bradford, "take off your pants" I shouted, Bob flicks two barrels to encourage him, "take them off ya daft cunt, eh you what" Bob can't help himself, he looks confused but drops his pants like he is about to get a free blow job, "all the fucking way" I throw the pants to Frank, "they go where the cases go." 1 minute 10 seconds past. By now the alarm will have been triggered and the guard is standing in his boxer shorts giving us full cooperation, it was almost like he was a pal.As Bob backs off for a split second I see it, the moment that has been haunting me all my life, a silhouette, it's Bob standing there unhinged holding two barrels, in the background a post office sign, what a devastatingly worrying sight, in a second I had captured an image that was almost a destiny for this lunatic.Frank has loaded the motor. 1 minute 40 seconds in. Bob is next, then before Chris leaves he blasts the tyres of the van, I think he just wanted to liven up the job to be fair, he's in the motor then me at the wheel, I was not letting Frank drive, this fucker had crashed more cars than Nicki louder!We're off steady away, 1 minute and 58 seconds, perfect. We head to the second car who was waiting patiently a few hundred yards away, the switch was fast and the first car torched and now we need to get back to the lock up.The battery life on the belt had a shelf lifeand this would trigger the cases. The journey home was quiet, we all had to let our hearts get back to reality, Bob seemed exceptionally calm, in an anxious world. In the lock up we had to grind the boxes open from the hinges, and tip out the cash from the bottom couldn't risk them going off, we stacked up the notes and tossed the cases to one side, only to hear them go pop twenty minutes later. "Fuck me that was close, you pair of clever cunts how the fuck did you know that was gonna happen" Frank laughed looking at Chris they both burst out laughing, this info cost us ten large but when you're staring at a hundred thousand sheets, it was worth it.

The job hit the news and this was a secret that stayed within our circle, who needed to know, no fucker I wasn't putting my freedom in the hands of some kingpin who wants to stay on the outside of the big fence, our arses were not about to be floated on the Teesside stock market and we certainly were not about to be carcasses for the ever circling criminal vultures. The cash had to go, so we sent that to Scotland to stay with family, it was safe up thereand we had to just be ourselves laying low.We had to take into account that quite possibly our collars were gonna get felt for this one it was all part of the deal.

"AT TIMES WHEN BOB'S KICKED OFF ON THE WING WE KNEW THAT ONLY ONE MAN COULD CONTROL HIM SO WE'VE HAD TO HELICOPTER DAVE IN TO CALM HIM DOWN. YES, IT WAS A COSTLY EXPERIMENT BUT I VALUE THE SAFETY OF MY STAFF MORE THAN GOVERNMENT MONEY."

HOLME HOUSE GOVERNOR

7

The Midlands Connection

So, here we are once again, even though it was a short visit they had nothing but a hunch and a gut feeling it was us, can't get a sentence on a hunch from a disgruntled police officer who isn't getting his own way.This guy was like a spoilt child, knocking on our door every time something popped up with two barrels. We knew we had to play ball, that was what Bob and me were good at, going with the flow, our legal team reassured us that a little time on remand that's all it would be. I mean the cheeky bastards refused bail on the grounds that we were 'a danger to the public,' with no evidence at all, but then hotel HMP wasn't really an issue and when our brief told us this Bob said "you kidding? Al punch your fucking head in ya mong."

I give up, we loved the fucking public if anyone was a danger to normal folk is was the likes of Carta and his bent lot, but this was how it was. Frank and Chris in Durham, me and Bob in Cumbria, which wasn't the best place for us to be but wedidn't give a fuck.Armed robbery with a possible ten large was our tag, that's all people needed to know, any problems see Bob.

Making new friends was what we did best, if we trusted them they would know and getting recognised for that little stunt in the club in Carlisle wasn't a good idea, too close to home here, something we had not taken into account whilst on our way to Haverigg.

The drama was to unfold in a sharp encounter in the gym, outnumbered and facing a defeat didn't sit well "how marra big Kev sends his love" this was shouted across the sports hall anonymously from a group of five or six, "Bob, I think big Kev is that daft cunt at the club" I laughed out loud but I was fearing the worst here, Bob was wanting to do what he does best, he wanted to windmill into the fucking lot of them, we would have lost here but two of them would have got hurt, even that was a victory, "eh you what?" Bob yells back across, nothing was putting him off here. Bob shouts again "you what gobshite, al punch your fucking head in ya mong." There was a long stare and screws were on to it, "now you two, we will have less of that" typical, a fucking Geordie screw, pointing his stick right at me, then out of nowhere this fella comes over, "alright lads, this bunch of shit houses couldn't fight themselves, I'm massive" Bob was weary, and turned to him sharply, "steady big man, that's my name Massive" he laughed and held out his hand and was well in our space this kid had balls, there was something about him that was safe, we shook hands, it was a firm grip you can tell a lot by a handshake and when that Cumbria lot seen this they disbursed from the gym rather fast, turns out the guy called massive had a fair crew in here. "Massive, is that really your tag?" Bob laughed, we all laughed, "yea you want some big man, am just kidding" he was a good guy on the face of it, told us he was from the Midlands, some music and rave promoter a bit of a big deal in his own part, poor guy was stitched up by some cunt in his city, "there's nowt worse than being stitched up" Bob moaned.We hated that more than anything, we had come to despise anything to do with disloyalty and mistrust, probably because of what happened to our Frank a few years back with the so called people he trusted.

Over the time we spent in Cumbria, Massive and his pals become good friends of ours, he backed us to the hilt in any bother we had inside striping one of the Carlisle shitbags that belonged to 'Big Kev' was easy, people wanted a piece of Bob and me in there but they would have to get through the Massive ring of steel. He would often sit for hours talking about the bloke who put him inside and wanting him to suffer. "This wanker sounds like a right knob" Bob was almost as enraged as Massive, "he's off his nut your man Bob," laughed Massive, "mate you don't know the half of this cunt," I said rolling my eyes like I was Bob's Dad. "Ere you know what I have an idea," Bob pipes up with a huge smile, now when this cunt has an idea it's usually fucked up and dangerous. "Fuck off you" I kicked his leg and gave him the look that said think about what you're saying. "No really, when we get out, why don't we pop down and see Massive have a night out," Well there was nothing dangerous there, it sounded like a great idea. Massive sits up "wicked idea man, I will look after ya." This we already knew, he was genuine we could sniff out a fake from a mile, then Bob adds to the mix, "and whilst we are there we can take care of that little problem you have, no one knows us down there we can put this cunt away, as a favour." The conversation tone lowered and I couldn't help but agree, Massive sat back, gave it ten seconds smiled and yelled, "yes my man" with a sly grin he knew that if anyone could sort this mess out, these two crack pots from up north could.

We left that old shit hole soon after and if his trial went ok Massive would follow a month later, we liked him and we kind of owed him and a promise is a promise.

We battled alongside him and his boys on many occasion, he would laugh when me and Bob got into full swing he thought we were unstoppable. Our legal team had pulled through, all charges were dropped, no evidence to link us to the van job or whatever they had was weak. Frank and Chris spent a little more time in Durham, they had other shit going on, me and Bob needed a bit of down time.

Things in the town were brutal, the nightlife was a gunfight at the O.K. Corral. Bob was bashing mutant bastards daily and we had the bizzies crawling all over us after our release, fuming.

We had some money stashed from that last job but we couldn't touch it, it was red hot and we didn't know if we were being watched.Talking in code over the phone was easy when Frank phoned from Durham.Nine o'clock meant three o'clock, everything else was the opposite to what was said, sounds complicated but it wasn't really.

Back to work, we had money we pulled from an old job and Massive our man from the Midlands was released, he wanted us to go through and see him, so that was our down time, he threw a bit of VIP treatment for us in one of his clubs, champagne and all the trimmings you know how it goes, we're talking roped off area and three security, it was like a scene out of Scarface and we were Manny and Montana, guests of Sosa. It was to be best behaviour from me and Bob, this lot were sound. Scott, he was a character, was on trial for murder and attempted murder in Birmingham, half way through the trial all the prosecution witnesses vanished.Then there was john, he was villain from the old code, we met him with Massive he was finishing off a ten stretch for armed robbery. Ash he was some big shot pro boxer that had every door in the fucking Midlands, he was a gentleman and a loose cannon. This lot were like family and we were like royalty in this place.Massive really was a big deal around these parts, was hard to believe that some idiot stitched him up, so we had the best night ever, we loved the attention and partied hard, we got down to business, the second reason we were in Midlands was to take care of a little problem as promised.

Fright night...

After a brilliant weekend and a tour of the clubs, bubbly on tap, we said our goodbyes and swapped more respect with this firm than the whole of Teesside could ever give us.Well, I suppose that happens when you bash every cunt in town.These were good people and were to become lifelong brothers, we needed them to believe we had left town, only Massive knew we had checked into a hotel, part one was set, "nice one boys we'll see you soon." I gave out hugs and we were off, well just half a mile down the road.

Later that night Massive joined us for a quiet one and to chat about this cunt who put him away, "am goanna ring this cunts neck" Bob raged, "easy Bob am not going away for life" I was quick to add that bit.Massive laughed "can't thank you enough lads, if this goes right he'll be leaving the club scene that's for sure." We just needed to scare him enough to know his life was worth fuck all. Massive left us and went somewhere where he could be seen, visible to all. We had a couple of hours kip, then we headed over to the club where this bloke was going to be, we had masks and Bob brought two barrels, it was a risk but what the hell. "Bob listen to me we need to fucking scare him, is that clear? We aren't here to kill anybody ok?" I spelled this out like a fucking English teacher before an exam, "yea man course" Bob was pissed at this cunt, he hated a grass.

Outside the club he promoted and co-owned we waited, we knew everything about this bastard and he never even knew we existed. "There he is Bob, wait til the doormen go," I whispered to Bob who was impatient "ok." He pulled away from the club in his 4x4 alone and we edged out two cars behind him, it was steady we needed the other cars to disappear, it was 03:20, cold and the fog was slowing us down, up ahead a set of lights on red, he is right in front of us, we both stop all you can hear is the crunch of the tyres on the loose pebbles on the road, the mist hugs the motor and is making it impossible to see. Bob pulls down his mask cradling two barrels, he slips out of the car, the lights still on red not a soul in sight, he creeps alongside the jeep, opens the passenger door and quickly takes a seat, this bloke has turned white as Bob holds a finger to his own lips like a school teacher to her pupils and says "shhhhhh, drive." He's staring down the nostrils of our trusty two barrels, as he pulls away "oh my god what the fuck do you want?" He asks Bob with fear in his voice. Bob says nothing, which even I would be scared of. I overtake the jeep and Bob tells him to follow the car. By now this cunt is offering fortunes to let him go.

We pulled into a disused yard that we checked out the day before and turned all the lights out, my mask is down, we hood this Bastard so he can't see fuck all, and calmly take him out his motor, now we had made friends in jail with allsorts of people and my scouse accent was on point, Bob was to keep quiet and in my best scouse velvet tone I whispered to this trembling wreck, "do you know why we're here lad?" Piss running down his leg, "no no do I fuck please don't kill me" Bob shoves two barrels under his chin hard, "we think you have been a bad man" again in my best Liverpudlian tone, he falls to his knees and Bob pushes him to the ground, his hands in the prayer position, "please" he cries begging for his life.Bob drags him to the front of his jeep and lays him next to his front wheel, still hooded I take an old tyre out the boot, Bob revs his engine and I gently roll the tyre onto his head "Jesus Christ" he cries like a baby, I had to do it this way, I couldn't trust Bob on the clutch. The engine roars as the tyre tickles his face, this went on for a few minutes, Bob kills the engine. "Now you listen to me lad, I am only gonna say this once, do you ere?" I whispered real close. "Yea yea just let me go I have a baby," "you did a very bad thing to someone that I think the world of, it cost him dearly, do you understand me lad? "Jesus Christ please" again he begged for his life, "you put that right ok, because if I have to come all the way back ere from Liverpool again, I will pop you like a grape, and Trisha your bird, she will be marked lad ok?"

At this point, I was even scaring myself, and a silhouette of Bob with two barrels resting on his shoulder against the moon, was a sight I will never forget, our man on the floor shook like a dog in a winter yard, he was covered in his own piss, "you gonna remember lad?" "I will burn you mate, do you hear?" We lose the tyre and take off his hood, I wanted him to see Bob against the moonlight, this cunt looked in a bad way, Bob stood over him in silence, extended his arm with the cold black steel at the end pointing straight at his forehead, there was a pause, Bobs eyes widened, "oh fuck no" he stuttered in a broken tone, I stood him up only to bash him back to the floor, we have kept him here half hour or so, we were serious and he knew that.Bob took two barrels and like a kid on Christmas day his face lit up underneath his ski mask, boom he blasted his wheel and then the engine block.This shit bag was curled up in a ball, screaming he was no good. "There won't be a next time will there lad?" I mumbled in his ear, "no no please," he quivered like he was freezing cold. We have to leave now fast, I grab the briefcase out of the passenger footwell of his motor and leave him in a pool of his own vomit and piss.We're off, straight onto the motorway and am guessing by the time this cunt sorted himself out we were northbound. "Jesus man what the fuck was that I frightened myself there" we shared a laugh but it was packed with nerves and all we wanted to do was get back to our shithole and have a drink.We were too hyped to even think about the suitcase we grabbed that wasn't even part of the plan, two barrels needed a clean and she needed to go to bed, the false plates needed to come off at the next lay-by, and we needed to call Massive and check-in.

The best feeling in the world was knowing nobody in Teesside knew what we had done, that blue giro was too tempting for these bigwigs round here, our work would never end up in the hands of wrong doers.Often the people smiled right at us, by now though we knew who these people were, their names are being passed around the place like a pipe at a party.You see this is where the boys in blue have the upper hand, they find themselves a source which is the easy bit, this place is a marketplace for cheap punks selling, it's a bit like walking through an orchard and picking whatever apple you want, the source then becomes a bitch for a handful of blue boys and are allowed to, within reason, sell whatever to whoever and live like a king on land he thinks he owns confidently.

All sounds great doesn't it, well it's a bit like riding on the back of a lion, while you're on the beast hold on tight you will be fine, if you get off, you will get bitten, it's not about how many of these people in Teesside exist, it's how many there are per square yard.Remember this place produced one of the biggest supergrasses across the world, right here on one of our council estates, so don't be fooled by Teesside, it breathes like a dragon, an expendable one because they need to feed the mouth that looks after them and not let the fire go out and that's when low level shitbags become a target, random doors getting uninvited visits, using their own special key to gain entry, the real clever bit is, it's the law who leaks the source amongst the hyenas, turning the industry on itself creating paranoia, self-doubt, mistrust, envy and jealousy, the psychology is perfect like the place becomes a huge board game and the giant players are being paid to play, are there winners, or losers I doubt it.You only win if you don't play, if you do play your own game with your own rules and let nobody else join in, it's like playing wallie.That Teesside game where you simply kick a ball at the wall, keep it simple because if you let two or three people kick your ball it will end up in someone else's garden, you see not everyone knows how to kick the ball, the people I talk about are the people that want to join in your game, they want to kick your ball into the garden, then move onto the next game.

I know this all sounds like hell on earth in the criminal world but there are plenty of good businessmen here, plenty to trust so don't fear it's just how it is and the trick is to find out who is who and we did that fairly quickly, with the help of some experts.

So, with that in mind, it was always a good idea to keep cards very close to our chest, getting back home and opening the briefcase was a bonus this was an unplanned part of the job, call it a little side wage because there was eight grand in there "fucking get in" and not a soul knows about it or us" shouted Bob as he took a hammer and chisel to the combination locks, we agreed to put some money aside for Chris and Frank for when they got out, look after your own that's what we do and this was free money.The money in Scotland needed to stay there for at least six months.

Three days after we got back from the Midlands we gets a call from our new brother Massive, he had seen our work in the local newspaper and on their local news channel, 'Local businessman kidnapped beaten and robbed' "fuck me lads word on the street here is he's lost the plot and pulled out of half the venues, fucking nice one" he roared down the phone "you're a couple of top blokes the pair of ya have the freedom of our place anytime," he was serious, we done him a huge turn and his rival wasn't going to bother him again that's for sure, he received an anonymous text two days later simply saying "fair enough."Massive was to assume this was him acknowledging what had happened and why, as for me and Bob well it was business as usual, Frank and Chris soon got their release and we all partied, with that money that was free we decided to take a trip to Spain and Frank had a little business out there for us which was to last three weeks, the wage was fat but so was the risks. We had everything set up bags packed sunglasses ready then the phone rings.

The call...

We knew that this place was full of tough nuts, one name that kept popping up time and time again was 'BigBri.' Now, this fucker was trouble all on his own but we're not arsed about him but felt we needed to avoid him as much as possible.We knew that if we were to take on the place full time he would be an obstacle, he would certainly get in the way and our paths would definitely cross. So, I set about working on a plan to see where things stood with this bloke, he was heavy into the taxing game and am not talking about the Inland Revenue either. Bob always wanted to tax him as a show of strength we needed him to take his game elsewhere, we needed to give him a reason to pause. Now Bri had heard of us, whispers in the Teesside corridors of the clubs and pubs were getting louder, I think he was curious, he wanted a meet up but we had no time for coffee and negotiations over land, Teesside was ours already.We weren't about to a deal, this isn't Brexit, if this big cunt wanted a slice it was gonna cost him!

We saw big Bri as a hurdle, a checkpoint and every now and then he would be seen driving past one of our clubs in a Sierra Cosworth full to the brim, arms and legs spilling out of the windows, being followed closely by the old bill, the suspension crying like a baby, carrying a hundred and twenty odd clem of pure machine.

It was during an afternoon gym session that the call came in, it was Bri, he wanted to meet up strangely on a school field in the middle of nowhere so this was our call, the conversation on the phone was polite, inviting, and predictable this mountain was not about to get his paws on Bob, or me, if he wanted a slice of Teesside's finest he would have to take us both or no deal.

So, it was arranged, best vests and joggers and we're off in separate cars,I had two barrels in the boot. Bob was fired up arriving at the school field to what looked like half of England, standing in the circle was a giant shadow boxing, hands all tied up, Bob leaps out of the motor alone and I am yards away but right by his side, we give each other the nod and begin our stroll towards the barbaric hoard, this was our moment, we were about to make Teesside ours officially, big Bri was about to work for us.

We unzip our hoodies and like synchronized swimmers drop them to the floor, we head towards the arena to crowds cheering "come on Brifucking do them" the circle gives way to make an opening for us. I don't like this at all, there were more ghosters in this crowd than in heaven, Bob is on his toes, I am too, Bri beckons us forward with both hands, an invitation we cannot refuse. Bob's hands are up as mine are too "come on" shouts Bob, there's a little dance as we analyse his moves. Bob ducks,Bri lets go the first shot, he's windmilling, looking like the blades off a chinook, "fuck sake" mutters Bob, he misses and I am in, I throw ten thousand right hooks that sweep over the top of this giant, "come on" Bri teases us forward, we clash like mountain goats, the crowed closes in but Idon't like this, this lot are his crowd not ours, as we break once more all three of us are eager to get the job done, this is serious business the stakes are higher than pally park.More hands are let go, sharper than a blade, the crowed are like animals wanting blood, "come on Bri" they want this over with.Bri's vest is torn, I have a graze, Bob wants this, but there is the familiar sound of sirens, dogs barking and radios talking shit. "It's the law" someone shouts from the crowd and they all split like ants, leaving the three of us standing there, breathing heavy, staring at each other with more unfinished business than the Tories, surrounded by police dogs yelling at us, all wanting a bite fuck out of our troublesome flesh.

Bri holds up his hands, we follow "easy lads, we're all pals here right lads" Bri shouts, "yea well aye" Bri holds out his hand to offer a fake shake, to get us out of what was about to be a tricky situation and as a show for the boys in blue, we have to agree, this handshake was firm, and seemed to last 5 hours, this meant nothing, or did it?

Three men in vests and the law could prove nothing but our names, they knew who we were and why we were here, "what's going on here Brian?" asks a copper holding a dog that wants a close up of our throat, "fuck all we're just talking" Bob mutters, "well I want you all out of here in ten seconds, is that clear" "I was quick to agree, "you're the boss" as we all part amidst the GermanShepards mouthing off and the sound of Bri's crowd in the background, there is an unspoken silence, this bloke was huge but you know what, we turned up, just Bob and me, and Bri knew that.Like the fight in the scrap yard with Frank and Woods, we never turned down the invite.

We were about to become the chat of the social clubs on a weekend, the shit talk in the kitchens on a Sunday morning amongst piles of dust, people telling their own version of what they saw that afternoon like some storyteller in a nursery classroom, with a dozen or more scaffs sat on the floor with milk and a cookie all eager to hear the tales of the Teesside rumble in the jungle and as the seasoning gets added the fight becomes more spicy, Bob and Dave took on the mountain.

The truth is that it doesn't matter what version of the event you hear, what shot landed or what shot missed, big Bri was shaken that's for sure he was expecting a no show, what happened that day was never settled, maybe we will let him have another shot at the title, maybe we wouldn't need to. We had to get on with our work, we had a town to run next stop a job in the sun.

"WHEN I COME IN PRISON I OWN THE TELEPHONE SYSTEM".

BOB

8

Costa Hell Sol

So we head off for our holiday job, shit shirts and ray ban's in the top pocket, all I had to do was keep Bob on a fucking lead, I had to get it into his fucking skull that we had a job to do out here and not to do a fucking Teesside bomb in the pool at every opportunity. The job seemed easy enough a rich couple of ex-pats living the good life in Spain had been getting threats of extortion and kidnap, so all four of us were tasked with the babysitting job.

The couple were really nice 'Steph and Jackie' they were a bit shook up, we just needed to look after them until they moved from Spain to another island, that was the story anyway three weeks and they were off.We got to know them well fairly quickly and it was about trust, they need to trust us, well this was our bread and butter we pulled trust off fast. "Piece of piss this Frank,"Bob whispered, Frank laughed and replied "don't get too comfy kid these fuckers round here don't know us, so if it goes off, it goes off bigtime" he laughed some more and looked at Chris, who was already laughing "we'll be sound here lads sunshine all day" Chris didn't give a fuck about anything but I kind of did the real processing thing and realised we weren't even in our country but then thought, I am with Frank, Chris and Bob and that's all I would ever need in any war.

The couple were happy to see us and wanted to be seen with us around where they lived, so we got set up. Me and Bob went for a walk to the local town to get familiar with the place.Bob stops to buy a drinkand to practice his shit Spanish. "olla" shouts Bob in his finest Teesside tone, the bloke just looked at him like he was on a rape charge, he quickly followed it up with "ere a said olla, al punch your fucking head in ya mong" now we have a standoff with the

Spaniard, who didn't know Bob and didn't give a fuck to be fair against Teesside Bob, we only wanted a drink. I got in between them and reminded Bob where we were, "a don't give a fuck, eh you what?" we left under a barrage of Bob and Spanish verbal, we had only been here an hour fuck sake.

We got back to Frank and Chris, and the place where we were staying.We had a small villa close to theirs, they needed us round the clock five days a week on weekends they were off out the country, so we took shifts, me and Bob would do a couple of days then Frank and Chris would do through the night, then we would swap, "I fucking love it here me" Bob shouted from our pool, "Icouldn't agree more bro, come on let's get sorted we're on shift in one hour, I think Steph wants to pop into town, look sharp" I shouted back. "Who ya talking to al punch ya fucking head in" Bob yells back then starts to laugh. I hadn't heard that for a while, made me laugh as long as it was in jest.

I remember this day it was belting, thirty degrees, we had our own car it was Stephs, convertible we always travelled separately and Bob always liked to drive, "so how the fuck did we end up like this, we were locked up a few months ago" I had to just remind Bob and laugh, Bob and me, in Spain, wearing our favourite vests, traps out, driving a flash motor with the roof down and both wearing smokeylenses,and the best bit is we're being paid, every time we spoke about it we would just laugh uncontrollably. We stop at the lights, Steph and Jackiein front, the sun is doing its best to melt the fresh pale skin of the two new meatheads from the up, the lights are on red, from nowhere a tall man in a t-shirt approaches Steph at his side window, Bob nudges me but I am already on to it, he says something in Spanish which Steph understands, now this guy did not look like your average holiday Spaniard he was more worn in, skin like that shite suede jacket Frank stole from C&A last year, he begins to rummage around in his pockets, I had seen enough, I leap out of the car without opening the door and approach the man, my left arm putting some space between him and the car whilst making eye contact with Steph. "You ok Steph?" I whispered while keeping this guy in the corner of my eye, "errmIdon't know Dave, I don't know him and he's a bit" I had heard enough, turned and dropped this fucker like a dumbbell that was too heavy, he falls to the ground and out from nowhere comes another,I trade with this one he's not local and can take a shot, we needed to get out of here remembering we aren't in Kansas no more Dorothy. "Steph go" I shouted, they were off and Bob filled their place in a flash, I throw myself into the car and we screeched off seconds behind them. "Let's go back al punch fuck out of every single one of them" Bob rages but we were not here to cause a war, we were here to do a job. "Stay behind Steph Bob let's not freak them out." We raced through the town like cannonball run, after a mile or so things were slowing down and we re-grouped back at the villa.It wasn't until then I had realised the cunt had cut me, it wasn't deep but it was five inches,I never even seen it, "fuck sake" I stamped my foot annoyed that I didn't spot the blade, "am gonna punch that cunts head in" Bob shouts he was furious, but that was done and Ididn't need stitches so we are all good. Steph and Jackie were safe but very shaken and apologetic, "you two ok?" I asked, we thought they were just a couple of well off frightened ex-pats, our suspicions were clarified soon after they explained that it wasn't a random attack.

The two muppets I put to kip were part of a crew that lost half a ton of powder a month ago, these two were moving more pills and marching powder in Spain than Lloyds pharmacy, these fuckers were as big as it gets and their yacht that sailed around the island wasn't making random stops for nothing to see the sights now was it. "We're ok and thank you" Jackie quivered and Steph took hold of her "it'sok"he whispered, "I just can't wait to get the fuck out of here Steph." Frank and Chris heard the commotion and when Steph and Jackie weren't looking, laughed like fuck, this went on for days with no let up. Frank and Chris got into a situation too, close to the villa.They leathered three strangers with a pole for taking an interest in Stephs car, things were very strange and uncomfortable even for us. We had battled men that looked like CharlesBronson or BurtReynolds, I had been slashed, Frank lost a tooth, and Chris broke a finger. Bob, well all he did was complain that he never got any scars.

The next shift was on the yacht, it was one of our last jobs, me and Bob boarded, Frank and Chris were already on board, in the hull there were two Spanish geezers tied up and mouths gagged.I looked at Chris, Bob looked at Frank, they're both stood each holding a pistol, Frank flicks the end of his baseball cap with the barrel of his 9mm, "alright kid?" he smiled and let out a puff of air "the fuck?" laughed Bob like this was some sort of joke. Frank laughed "we're out of here tonight kid, last job" he whispered.This fucking boat was full of twenty five years in a Spanish jail and did we give a fuck, four Teesside nut jobs maybe should have but didn't, this was the biggest tax you ever did see and we were to be well looked after.

After this we needed to be out of the place timing was everything, Steph and Jackie sailed to the other side of the island, our job was to keep the two prisoners scared, offload the goods then dump the boat, "how the fuck do you dump a boat?" Bob asked, seemed like a fair question to me.We were to anchor it two miles out to seaand a smaller speed boat would bring us back. Frank and Chris pissed themselves, they knew all along this was the big one but they didn't want to panic us, "they did alright these two" Chris howled and Steph joined in the conversation "they fucking did like, al give them that" they weren't a couple of frightened ex-pats, these fuckers were big time drug barons, this taxing yachts malarkey happens a lot apparently. Steph lost one last month to a load of French pirates, it's tit for tat over here, we wondered how we got this job, turns out Frank had met Steph in jail some time ago, it all made sense now, the little cunt, but Bob and me gave no fucks and we did what we had to do.

We needed to pack the fuck up and leave Spain, the two sailors were left on board tied up just before leaving Bob gave his usual speech "ere olla, daft cunts if I find out you have untied yourselves before we get out of here, al punch your fucking heads in," pointless speech really as they couldn't speak English and Bob liked to finish any work with a bit of Bob.

We dashed off in a speed boat like a couple of rubbish MI5 agents and made our flight, got the fuck off this soil.Me and Bob did not want to imagine the jail we had left behind but we got well paid and earned respect you could only dream of. Frank just winked at the airport this was his way of showing nerves, we never took any of this shit back to Teesside, not a chance we didn't have to be told we had learned that much over the years, we took more money than we knew what to do with but that was never on show either, too many spiteful jealous, greedy excuses for plod, there were sentences being dished out around Teesside like perfume samples in boots, we were not about to become some cunts lighter bird time, our exploits were not some wankers currency to trade with so it was back to normality as quickly as possible. Our cash stash in Scotland was building up nicely, and as far as anyone knew we had simply been on holiday.

The Teesside pecking order...

Back to normal and that meant gym and work, this place just gets better, I mean there are people getting locked up, tough guys pissing up lampposts on estates like dogs marking territory and you can almost see other tough guys squirming as they pick up on the scent left behind.

Their stories doing the rounds, being hurled about like a hot potato, getting passed to the next gobshite, by now we had heard thirty different versions of the fight with me Bob and Bri.Weekends and nights out are becoming fake battle grounds as top dogs attempt to take on the next top dog from the next estate, the cling on's who are out and about needing photographs to prove their loyalty and to warn off other cling ons, I know this sounds complicated but it's a simple science really, getting a photo with a tough guy means you're doing ok, really, no it's worthy of a giggle and a cringe, our job was to stop the battlegrounds being on our premises, it was usually not that difficult, you show them respect and they give it back in abundance, a mean these fellas like the front of queue treatment, they love the "get yourself straight in lads" and if you waver the two pound entry fee well this is a mark of true honour.These people have money coming out of their arse ends, it's not about two quid it's the 'nod' the 'wink' the little tap on the chest, we gave and received the same invisible honour as these folk, they called you names like "mush" or "chore" or even "son" yea I know, fucking son. I recall a time Bob and me were earning extra cash on a place we were working, here is how it works.The place is rammed, I mean the greedy little bastard owner was breaking all the rules here if the fire brigade turned up the place would have been closed but hey, we just did what we were told, so we're down to one in one out and this place was popular, anyone who is anyone in here the queue spills out onto the street like an overflowing sink, looking down the line needing binoculars to see the last man, it was a fiver in, but me and Bob charged our own fiver to come to the front of the queue, so technically it was a tenner to get in and we got half of the money, brilliant I know. Then across the street the obligatory bunch of scaffs that have been on the piss all day, this lot are like one big happy family, all looking the same with their stripy jumpers, and their timberland boots, each one with his own eight ball tucked away somewhere, these guys don't care that there is a bag of dust mixed in with their loose change, oops, the way round that is to offer you a line n all tha, we know it's them because their voices arrive before they do, deeper than the canyon, we're not sure why the voice drops on Teesside hard cases, our theory is that we think it's primal and when you're a tough guy, it just happens unfortunately.

So there's plenty of swear words and calling each other affectionate names like 'daft cunt', or melt, all talking about the same shit, mixed together with the mandatory, stomp arms waist high, going up and down like a windup toy, these boys are very hands on, headlocks and slaps are a way of showing love to each other and as a special treat if you're really lucky, there will be a couple of boxers in the group doing pad work, without gloves on bare hands, it looks cute, but we never have quite understood this practice, it's normally used as a greeting when other scaffs meet other scaffs, it's straight on the pads at the bar, you need to see it to make your own mind up. This lot will disregard the queue and the fact that there are dozens of people who have been stood waiting, its straight to the front and all we can hear is "ere ereere, where's Bob go" and "get Bob or Dave" in the deepest of tone, whilst climbing all over each other like a "all pile on" game at school, slapping the apprentice on the back of the head, I mean this is part of the young man's training, he observes and overnight transforms into 'a scaff', this is actually how they're born. So amongst the rattling of gold chains and bracelets, and after one of them gives out the odd "fuck you looking at?" to the bloke in the queue who can't quite believe what he is seeing, one in one out but in go six scaffs after slipping a purple note in the handshake and the no fucks given, even the obligatory offer of "you wanna line kid" it is a done deal.They get a quick lecture about behaviour and make promises they absolutely cannot, and will not keep, it isn't there fault its just how it is when you're a clone, and in they go.

Folk in the queue are fuming but what can you do, we love the scaffscan't say no more about that and we can't keep everyone happy. Then out of nowhere from the bar next door comes the well-dressed tough guy, on his own treating his beautiful girlfriend to a night out, a mean she is stunning, batshit crazy and very tolerant of her bad boyfriend, this guy is looking sharp and so is she, nice crisp shirt maybe from Moss bros, with cufflinks, maybe a waistcoat and stinking of creed. Now this fella when he's with his boys is a completely different person, blowjobs in a back alley n all tha, the lot, he wants her to see how well behaved he is when he is out, he could be a scaff that sells on the side in disguise, but tonight he's a gentleman, he's quiet and respectful.He has usually been for a meal over candles and talked of love whilst texting his side piece under the table with his toes.They eat in that nice place normal folk avoid because they appreciate the value of the pound, all this is paid for by cash covered in dust, his sense of entitlement is world trade centre high, which means hers is too, she's spent nine days getting ready for tonight and is the best dressed doll in Teesside.

Now, for him this could all go wrong because Bob, me or Sean don't really give a fuck who or what he is, he is now relying on our good will and perfect timing, we make eye contact and it's all tense, under his tough shell he's weak, again it's straight to the front of the line, his hand gently on her waist as he nudges her in front of him, you see he is cleverly using her as collateral and a distraction, his puppy dog eyes are now speaking silently, they're saying 'don't let me down here big man, let's make this smooth,' on a good day, in a good mood a nod saves his life, because the back of queue would have finished him off and whatever reputation he has, through the crowd a firm handshake, a nice ring on the little finger and maybe a kiss on the cheek shows the gratitude, "what do you two want to drink?" with a sigh of relief bellowed over the loud music, we are happy.

Back outside the punters are whinging on but with no spokesman or shop steward, what can we do they just accept their place in the Teesside pecking order, it's like this if you want to be apex in this town or alpha, you got to at least pretend you're a big deal. So our job was all about managing the crowds, remember different estates have different germs and if we slip up and allow the germs to mingle then earning our money was inevitable, so keeping an ear to the ground and listening to which nuisance has chew with whoever was very important, it kept us sharp. Now we can't forget the sporty tough guys, this lot go out straight after a barbeque or some sunshine gathering, this lot all fuelled by the white devil, that means no food was consumed in the garden at all, this lot don't care that their faces look like a sherbet dib dab, with their jaw doing a dance all on its own, It might just be that they're sat in the house and decide last minute to go out on a Saturday night, now this lot are a thousand percent sure entry to the gaff is a done deal, because one of them will 'know Bob's mate, or Dave's cousin' so before they even set off, the confident one will have assured the rest of the Shitbags of this.

When they arrive they always attempt to flex their reputational muscles by arriving at the door straight to the front, I mean their disregard for humans is bizarre and callus, in Nike trainers, football or Bermuda shorts and white socks, they carry the same deep gravelly voice as the scaff, there always pissed and never show an ounce of respect for us or the job we're doing, so with that in mind they are shown the contempt they deserve, these boys don't understand the word contempt, that makes it even funnier, it wasn't uncommon for us to walk away from them halfway through a sentence, pure distain was our thing and we did it well, this always worked and drained the tough guy out of them, firstly they try the "ya fucking joking aren't ya?" arms out stretched approach, it was always met with "do we look like we're joking?" We are always polite and the answer was always absolutely no, now this lot persist and even try a different tact, what these idiots don't understand is, it's their clothes we have an issue with, it really is that simple, lowering their voices and suggesting we let them in through the side door was a common tactic, that never worked, but what does god love, there is no bullshit with me and Bob the answer is still no, after the humiliation, it would always resort to "it's fucking shite in there anyway" walking backwards with a thousand yard stare, then at a safe distance "wankers" from an anonymous member of the group, chancers and risk takers.

Then we have the dealers, this lot are usually well dressed, lots of gold sitting on their just pumped up that day traps, they move around really slowly like they're not in a rush, now these helmets give a little respect but want you to know that it is a favour, so you get the nod, if you're lucky you will get a handshake with a little extra squeeze, we think this is also primal, if you earn a wink you may get called son or even chief, these creeps always leave you gobsmacked and shaking your head, nothing a quick palm strike can't sort out, their numbers are small two or three because they're better than everyone else you see, these people always end up at a party uninvited, dragging the atmosphere with them from North Korea, they are unfunny and usually have the personality of a bronze statue, they spend big and buy your drinks all night with each visit to the bar a fresh note, they don't do change and hunting through a palm full of coins is, well just not happening, they usually drive a white Mercedes 'on lease known as the 'whiff drop', and rarely are these fuckers drunk, they arrive at the club in the whiff drop and want to be seen.

They move in slow motion and wear saddle or keeper rings bigger than their heads. Nobody is as impressed as they think, they're just a shit stain on the town. We can't forget the ladies that we like to call the 'medusa's', they walk past you like you don't exist, your simply the shit they have stood in, interestingly they never make eye contact with you, their faces have no expression at all, eye contact means you want them, now this lot hang out in groups of two or three, they usually match a specific wine with their meal in a country pub and talk about walking or their two children, their blokes are almost certainly smashing other women and this lot normally know about it, they're just too scared to act on it. Once in a while they venture to our place, just so they can look down their noses at the 'common people' to make themselves feel better about the imperfect lives they actually have. Now this bunch of females are so 'happily married' they use their fucking wedding rings as ID and flash it in your not interested face, like a rubbish Beyoncé and the very sound of a male voice causes them to cringe and come out in a rash, any attention from the opposite sex is met with the face of the 1970's flick Clash of the Titans Medusa, turning any man into stone instantly, this lot are best treat with the same contempt and attitude that they bring with them, usually the night ends with one of the group "asking to speak to the manager" because a local shitbag offered to buy her a drink, then called her a frigid bitch. They arrive happy and better than anyone on the planet and leave having their night ruined by a local moll who called one of them a stuck up slag for looking at her bloke, because secretly their unconscious desire is to have a little bit of rough.

Waiting patiently in the queue are the towns normal folk, they work hard and just want a good night out, they're never any bother and are always well turned out, the sad story about the normal folk is they're usually the cannon fodder, they have watched every shitbag in the town slip in the club before them and this has spoilt their night, first cunt that says a word to any of them is getting a mouthful, they're willing to speak their mind but sadly it's usually to the shite we have just let in and that becomes their problem. It's a vicious circle the Teesside pecking order, it all sounds like chaos but it works, although there is a level of acceptance, people don't like it one bit but they simply get it.

Shoot the trouble…

Trouble inside, once again this time it's me,Bob and our third fist Sean, now this bloke was black magic, his hands were sharp and his legs could fight all on their own, in we go, it's swimming with the salmon again, people getting knocked over for no reason, but that's how it goes.Now this brawl is in full swing, the crowd has even formed a ring to let them dance, me,Bob and Sean are like hyenas waiting to grab the carcass from the stuffed lion, all we need is a slight break, these two fuckers are still at it and the music is cut, there's a break, in we go Bob steps in and takes over the big guy and is now swapping shots, me and Sean latch onto this other fella like a couple of octopus and take him to the floor, we need him asleep and so I proceed to write this cunt a prescription for some night time meds.He's too big to deal with, I edge around to his throat and apply a sleep aid, but he's still wide awake. Sean has him tied up, "watch his legs Sean," I scream out this guy is strong, then out of nowhere Sean shouts out loud "it's ok Dave I have broken his thumbs," I remember thinking I didn't know whether to laugh or feel relieved that we were snapping people's limbs as a social compliance technique, he looked at me like he wanted a well done, I mean I gave him one but this was backward, my sleeping tablet was starting to take effect and Bob had finished the other guy and returned to help out. "Ok ok" he spluttered, the game was up, half asleep he was exited through the side door backwards, in the rain. Home time, a clever trick me and Bob used was anyone causing trouble in our place we would deliberately tear their shirt off their back, this would ensure home time and nobody else would let them in anywhere. Home time.

There's more commotion inside and in go me and bob, by the time we get there it's all over, folk are standing there with their arms in the air as a sign of innocence, all accept one, now this guy is an old school tough guy he still dresses like an old shite hawk, we clocked him on the way in and made the cunt pay, being an old bully who slaps women is not currency in our world, or our place so there was no love lost, "you get the fuck out or al smash ya lass again" Bob shouts in front of the whole world, there really is no need to manhandle this shit bag, throwing him out was enough to show what we thought of him, his protests were futile and his old entourage all followed suit and so did the young lad he just slapped on the dance floor, so this lot aren't giving us grief, there all outside in disbelief of their departure, out goes the victim and wants a piece of the old dog, I pull Bob back and whisper to him "let it go big man, this kid will finish his career" we both laughed as yesteryears Teessider is finished in seconds, then Bob always finished moments like this with "a wanna grand off ya" to the shitbag.

It's moments like this that make the night worth it, the money wasn't fantastic, we may have made five hundred after taxing and doing our own door payment scheme but the banter with the lads was priceless. The place is crawling with yesteryear boxers, football hooligans, and old criminals who have found some sort of moral compass, they're all good people with great stories to tell and a lesson or two can be learned from pulling up a sandbag and sharing a brew, but pissed up we have no time for old men that have spent twenty five years in Durham prison and have become self-styled Teesside Z listed celebrities with jobless ganja smoking younglings that look up to this bullshit, strutting around the place thinking their story is worth more than the pound.

Now,I do remember an elderly gentleman and his fucking great-grandsons kicking off one evening in our club, I say our club because we made more money than the club, so it was our fucking club and this was a big one, me, Sean, Bob and three others all toe to toe, I was clocked in the ear and I could hear Big Ben ringing for days "ya fucking bastard" I yelled like a bitch and Bob couldn't do nowt but laugh, the old man that orchestrated the whole thing looked like a nineteen sixties wife beater with a teddy boy, Bryl creamed, grey tobacco pissyLes Battersby hair do and sporting a smoke stained cardigan, furious outside because we dismissed his thousand year prison sentence for attempted murder back in seventeen thirty one, contempt was something myself and Sean could show with style.

I clocked his boy with a right and caught him before he hit the floor, "there you go shhhhhh, now come back another time you have had way too much to drink" I whispered into his ear like I was a hypnotherapist, he left asking what had happened and like Paul McKenna I re-told him my version of events, three two one you're back in the room.

"BOB'S BEEN MY BEST MATE SINCE WE LEARNT TO SWEAR AND SMOKED TOGETHER. DEEP DOWN HE'S AWFULLY SENSITIVE. PEOPLE ONLY KNOW OF HIS REPUTATION, THEY DON'T KNOW HIM LIKE I DO AND THAT'S WHY I'M THE ONLY ONE WHO CAN CONTROL HIM."

DAVE

9

Business is Business

Nights at work were funny and we kept them separate from other exploits, our work outside was always kept quiet, it's why we had success for so long, we invested our money slowly and carefully into property, we opened up our own Estate Agents subletting property's that didn't belong to us, when purchasing a property Bob would always make a 'Bob offer' which was take it or take it, or "al punch fuck outtaya," on Bob's housing market an eighty grand three bed mid terrace always went for oh, about thirty grand, and that was a good deal if you were selling. I let Bob do the talking in any money deals, he had a way with words, we spotted a nice place in a decent part of Teesside, away from the shite, this was to be our home, four bedroom detached, driveway, double garage that was on the market for one hundred and eight grand, which was a lot of poke in the early nineties.Bob arranged to view the place on a Sunday afternoon after the gym.The bloke selling was young, he inherited it off his grandmother, Bob did his homework. We pulled onto the drive and it looked nice, Bob has already made the offer in his head, he has already shook hands and is making alterations to the place before getting out of the car.The door opens and out pops this little squirt and greets Bob. Bob is straight in with "al give ya sixty grand for it ya daft cunt, al punch ya fucking head in" Bob shared his offer and wasn't leaving without a handshake.This bloke was gobsmacked.

Anything Bob wants to buy is only ever worth what Bob wants to pay, we learned this trick off Viv up in Newcastle. I mean that's forty eight grand below the price, the little cunt managed to get sixty two out of the big man, which was impressive,Bob was spitting feathers, "cheeky little cunt him, two grand he had out of me!" Bob moaned all day about this and missed the fact he robbed the poor kid out of a fortune, but that's business, that's how things were. If we needed a motor Bob would go straight in for less than half the asking and if the seller looked like he was about laugh, that would be met with Bobs negotiating skills.

These skills were hired on many occasions whether it was for collecting debts, or some couples therapy, Bob once told a bloke that if he didn't get back with his Mrs and stop being a shitbag, he would punch his fucking head in, they lived happily ever after.Debt recovery was always right down the middleof what we retrieved, ten grand for a punter then we kept five, our moto was half of something, was better than getting nothing.Our work was always out of town and usually for business owners, we had our own system and it worked well, it was called the 'hostage model' we tried to sell it as a training package to a company who trained bailiffs but apparently, there was an ethical concern with the branding, so here's how it works. Find the target who owes the money, identifying him or his company as the debtor, the hostage model is simple Bob would take stage one, this involves one sided demand for the money owed, something like this. "Listen daft cunt you owe XYZ let's say twenty five grand, and if you don't cough that up now al punch fuck out of you, and everyone you know, including your lass and your mam then al smash her." Game on, Bob now has his hostage, after a period I would then enter as the negotiator, at this point I am negotiating with both parties, Bob and the debtor, Bob isn't budging on his arrangement he would still want to punch fuck out of the debtor, but I would offer a solution to the little problem he has found himself in, like this "look we can all leave here safely, Bob if you just back off a little and let him think for a moment" the solution has toalways be more attractive, that's the key, something like that, it's a bit of a rebrand on the good cop bad cop, but we hated the word 'cop' we preferred 'hostage' so that was never gonna work and by the time I have put Bob back in the cage it always looked like I was doing the debtor a favour. We used Frank and Chris once to collect six grand from an ex-policeman who had a bit of a gambling habit.Ever have that feeling when someone just takes things a little too far, I wanted to use the hostage model, in every sense of the word. Frank ties this plod up and wants him to hear the whole story, of how his pals have been wrong uns, Chris howled, this plod was giving up names we weren't even asking for, "you have the money just leave me alone now, untie me and I will tell you who has been on the take for years" he moaned on and on, "let's hear it kid, untie him" I was curious and so was Chris, come to think of it we were all curious.

So like we were about to watch a movie we pulled up a chair and all listened, some of this stuff didn't surprise us, names, dates, places, but some of it did, "fuck off" I heard Chris mutter under his breath as he stood up in disbelief like he had seen a ghost. I had heard enough this ex old bill was spewing his guts up about every crook on Teesside. I already have the money in my hand "kid, kid come on I have the cash let's bail" business is business, and ex-copper or not this bloke had been a naughty boy he wasn't about to spill this one, and on the way out Bob blasted this car with old two barrels "fuck sake you and that fucking thing" I screamed, Frank jumped in and laughed like fuck "he's not well him kid" "tell me about it." Bobs Theory was he would have to explain his car being shot and that would be uncomfortable. The silence in the car on the way back spoke volumes about the place we lived in, some of it was really sad and yet unsurprising. With this new knowledge we were able to keep ourselves even more safe, we were able to keep people at a very long arm's length, both Frank and Chris had learned something that night that shook their world, maybe a friendship restructuring was needed, confident that all our work was out of town and on a need to know basis, was our best weapon.

With a decent portfolio building up we were doing ok, two dozen houses or so and rising, things weren't too bad we always had a different motor each month, names popped up now and then and were chucked at us like a snowball at playtime, names meant nothing to us and reputations were bullshit, unless we could see what you were made of, it was all shite. Harry Brown, or Harry 'the gun' as he was known, an old school doorman who had a few tricks up his sleeve and a few nasty surprises, he ran his mouth about Bob one night in his club, he was seen waving a blade around half cut like really crap Jack the hat before Ronnie and Reg got him. Alex H, or as we know him Alex 'The Hammer' a well-known gangster who always fancied a slice of Bob, he wasn't that tall and often carried something wherever he went, we knew nothing about him really, he bashed someone with a lump hammer once hence the name, tools were a sure thing with him, then there was Johnny and Richie, a couple of brothers who moved around Teesside, like the Krays only cheaper, these two were drama always in a suit, Bob wanted these two and it would have been messy, but these two took a wide berth around me and Bob.

DazRobo, this cunt was a ginger bastard that resented everyone who wasn't, he took his fucking scruffy genetics seriously, he based your friendship on the colour of your fucking pubes. This lot were all capable in their own rights but Bob always had a special message for this lot, his message was simple "al punch fuck out of every single one of them" I never doubted this and deep down neither did they. Keeping their distance and never actually confronting us worked for everyone, everyone had a lot to lose. If we were working, this bunch were drinking elsewhere, avoiding us like the Black Death, so there was an unspoken, unwritten rule, you keep out of our way and we'll not punch fuck out of every single one of you, we will let you live.

Rumours were doing the rounds that this lot were teaming up to teach Bob and me a lesson, well this wasn't happening Bob and I had a plan, pick these fuckers off one by one. We never took this seriously because none of this lot would take us face to face, but then Harry the gun was involved, and he was unpredictable. Around this time it wasn't uncommon for unmarked armed response to follow me and Bob around and once or twice a week the full Shabang, stop weapons drawn get out of the vehicle treatment, our names were on a lot of heat around the place, even in Newcastle when Bob and me were up to see Viv, we were followed from the fucking A19 and spun like a couple of terrorists, they knew who we were and even talked about our business with Viv "Viv who?" Asks Bob with his usual dumb look, "divent fuck aboot, you're in the toonnooya cunt" this copper meant business, and he knew we weren't here buying newkey brown, we had been questioned for an armed robbery in Durham and one in Skipton, in the same month, whenever we were stopped by the old bill it was always the full squad, weapons drawn the lot, we would laugh about how much it cost the force just to pull us over, we were smoking so playing games was not on our agenda at the moment, and this meant we couldn't carry anything, it was far too risky and going to war with Harry and Alex the hammer needed avoiding at all cost.

Through the day we watched our backs for the law then at night we were careful about where we were exposed, I phoned Bob before work one weekend as usual "Bob I will pick you up round the back, am being followed" I always felt uneasy without the big guy, so we switched ourselves on, Chris and Frank wanted to end this shit before it got off the ground their way, and Norman was sat with a shooter on his lap regularly, but we agreed to see how things unfolded over the week.

I picked Bob up and things were a little weird, we were never paranoid but something wasn't right about tonight, I was right about being followed and it wasn't the law, we were dressed for work and had nothing in the car but a bat, ball and glove and this 4x4 was three cars back poking its nose out of the traffic like it was sniffing the air, stay cool Bob we'll take them on a ride to see if they stay with us, we took random turns and meaningless exits with no pattern and there they were still three cars behind us, "right bob switch on, these cunts have a plan and we need one" I said quickly, this wasn't looking good these cunts had an agenda and we were it, I phoned Frank, he detected a panic "Frank where are ya kid?" He was onto it "what's up bro you ok?" He was on red alert "we're being followed kid and it's not the law," my voice wobbled and Bob was now up for it, he was fuming, but I had to use my brain, now he wants to pull over and have them but I knew these would have been carrying and so did Frank "don't pull over kid, keep them moving try and bring them to us" Frank had a plan "ok bro on my way".

At that the motor overtakes the three carsand drops in front of us, I don't like this my heart is pounding, I turn the stereo off and Bob is hyped, then in slow motion like some Hollywood bullshit we usually laugh at, their motor stops and is slammed into reverse, the tow bar was huge, it bashed the front of our wheels their back doors pop open and out jumps a little scroat wearing a filthy shell suit, all of seven stone wearing a mask, that was way too big for his tiny head, he's barely able to hold the two barrels that's at his waist, "fuck floor it" Bob shouts at the top of his voice, we're in reverse and moving backwards fast, with not a care for who is behind us, boom, boom, two shots, our windscreen has gone, we're showered in glass, but we are still going backwards I haven't even looked forwards I just want to get the fuck out of there, our back end slams off a parked car, glass is thrown everywhere, it's then I feel a sharp pain, and Bob isn't moving, "Bob Bob, wake up" I scream out loud and gave him a shove, "Bob, argh fuck sake" it's real we have both been hit but Bob is not with it, he's out, the 4x4 has fled and we are in a bad way, "Bob Bob fucking wake up." I remember hearing him moan, there is blood everywhere, our white work shirts were covered, it all went blurry and I passed out, I was in and out of conscious I remember hearing voices, the smell of the cold air, and warm blood, seeing blue lights, radios, my car door and roof had been cut off it was laying on the road side, I was carried into the ambulance with an oxygen mask on, "where's Bob?" I yelled, "it's ok relax, breathe" a friendly voice muttered I passed out again, I remember trying to put up a weak fight, "keep still" the ambulance man keeping me in my place, sitting up then falling back, "where's Bob?" I moaned. The next time I wake up I am in bed surrounded by police, I feel ok, just bandages and drips everywhere, "where's Bob?" It's all I wanted to know, then a doctor spoke, "he's in theatre, just relax." The police are itching to question me, so I just pretend to fall asleep again and they cleared off leaving two coppers behind, for now we were safe but what the fuck just happened. After I woke up Bob was in the bed opposite tubes everywhere and the sound of the beep beep machine, we weren't allowed visitors, "fucking Harry the gun" whispers Frank down the phone, this had to be his work, we heard about this weeks ago, he'd made the mistake of a lifetime. I just needed Bob to wake up and say something, even if it was to threaten a Doctor or anyone. As long as he wanted to punch fuck out of someone I knew he would be ok.

The plain clothes lot were back I knew they wouldn't let up, against the Doctors orders they just wanted names, they weren't stupid either, in strolls a confidant little gobshite "now then, listen you tell me it was Harry and Alex I will lift them tonight and get them out your way" with a smirk like he knew all about it, "I never seen fuck all and if you think it was them two, go get them what do you need us for?" I was still in pain clutching my ribs, "you're full of shit" he growled, I replied instantly with "ok boss" making eye contact with the Doctor and wincing was enough to get these idiots thrown off the ward.Me and Bob haven't got a fish and chip shop, we don't do helping the fuzz, we don't give information over to the blue boys, or any boys, even if it's about our enemies, no there is far too much of that going on already that isn't our bag am afraid.

I am worried about Bob I need him to pull through, he's across from me looking like an experiment in a Frankenstein film, where me am just bandaged up. Bob took the first shot and I took part of the second, who the fuck pulled the trigger, it's all coming back I remember he was a fucking little rat, probably a street rat pulling the trigger on me and Bob for a few hundred quid.

I recovered a few weeks earlier than Bob and that gave me time to put my ear to the ground, sniff around a bit to see what's what.Nothing, nobody was saying a thing Frank and his lot already kidnapped Harry Brown and he cried for days stating he had nothing to do with it, that left only one person crazy enough to pull a shooter on Bob and me, Alex H 'The Hammer', he hasn't been seen for weeks, we took doors off hinges on every estate looking for him, nothing, someone was hiding him and Bob knew that. Bob is on the mend so I go and visit I have nothing more than the names we already knew, he's conscious, and the machines are off, he is raging "What the fuck, who the fuck, tell me you know who fucked us over here?" Bobs spitting feathers "mate we're still in the hospital, shhhh" I whispered over the back of my hand, he wanted blood but everybody knew this, Bob wanted Norman and Frank involved and this would only mean one thing.

Double trouble...

Teaming up Frank and Norman was always going to be a combination of a force to be reckoned with, doors of dealers were being flattened and these two were not to be underestimated their similarities were uncanny, both explosive with an all in state of mind, on their own they were too much, together they brought way too much trouble, their escapades of late consisted of collecting everything from everyone. Two barrels each making people vomit in their own homes was quite a common practice. I remember a time both of them in the gym, in walks two guys both sporting two barrels, Frank gets one shoved in his face, Norm in his chest, there's a scuffle, people flee and the two brothers do what they do with a dumbbell and a curling bar, what a mess. Norman was regularly visited by murder squad detectives, over various events Norm wouldn't hand a single full stop to the police no matter what he knew he is made of pure principle right through.He once spiked a bunch of coppers in his flat with whizz whilst they tried to obtain information, "you want tea fellas?" he chuckled and waited for the conversation to 'speed up' he laughs about it still to this day. Norm and Frank had a bit of a habit of disappearing and turning up days later after some poor cunt turned up on the moors with their legs messed up, their work was signature in the underworld, if these two were your pals you were laughing, flip the coin and you're in a world of hurt. I recall that there has been a murder a young fella has been gunned down on the doorstep, in cold blood he was a close friend of our two, may have been really close who knows, even colleagues, our two vanished off to "visit family" in London that left this mess for me and Bob to sort out.

We were on our own with this one the others had enough on their plate, murder squad knocking on doors five times a day was always going to catch up with them. Harry had already had a visit from our lot that only left Alex. Bob had plans for Alex and Harry even though we now think Harry played no part.

Out of hospital but still in a little pain this shit needed sorting, we knew Harry would be the easier one to grab out of the two, so pub to pub we would pay a visit, turf didn't matter anymore, who's manor was who didn't make any difference at all, people knew Bob and Dave were on the move, so most shitholes were empty of villains.In we go and order a drink no alcohol this was serious, punters putting their heads down like we were medusa, only making eye contact with the carpet, and the beer stains that have lived there for decades, "now then" Bob mutters to the barman full eye contact, "alright Bob, Dave, what you lads doing round here" we sensed the nerves in his voice, like he was hiding a bank robber behind that bar, "you know why we're here ya daft cunt" Bob snaps, then lowered his voice and leaned into him, "now tell us where the old man is and Iwon't punch fuck out of ya" at this point I take over and help the poor lad out, then in a much kinder tone "look pal he is a bit upset and has been through a lot lately, tell him where the old boy is and I will buy you a drink and we will be off."

He lost the colour in his face and eventually slipped Bob an old betting slip, Bob laughed as he passed me the slip,"remember the last time some cunt did this kid" I couldn't help but remember that little moment in school, "haha yea the ghost."

I waited until the barman fucked off and opened the slip, there was a pub name written on it, a pub we knew but was not on our radar, we left and the drinks were paid for by some guy sat on his own in the corner, he waves and winks "say hello from me lads" he smirks. We flee the bar on a mission and head straight to this water hole, aware that the barman may have done a Smigga with the betting slip by phoning the place ahead of our arrival. This time we weren't bothered, we needed to talk to Harry tonight and we weren't even thinking about caution. Outside this idyllic looking place at the back of the car park there sits Harry's motor, looking as scared as him, so we know he's in, "right I will go in punch fuck out every single one of them" rages Bob "whoa mate, slow down" my voice of reason sometimes works on this occasion it did. The plan was we go have a drink and turn this fella into a funny shade of shit himself, always works so that's what we do.Walk in locate H, making eye contact would be enough to let him know why we were here, he spots us halfway through a mouthful, then grew six inches in his seat as the glass went down, I gave him a nod that nobody else could see, and three blokes stand up, now if you ever want Bob's attention in a situation like this, that's the way to do it, these idiots just invited us to the party, in no time at all it was time to dance.

Normal folk grabbed their drinks and coats and cleared off, Bob slips on a duster like it was a wedding ring and the wife just walked in, we do these three as quick as you can think about it. "Sit your fucking arse down" Bob shouts to Harry who was making a hasty retreat whilst three of his finest attended to their wounds, Bob turns to the three bodyguards and whispers "a wanna grand off ya" now H turned that colour we talked about, "lads lads" an out of breath Harry the gun whimpered, "let's go" I ordered him out of the bar and we all leave together amidst three barely alive henchmen, Bob shoving him in the back every few seconds "keep fucking moving, eh you what al punch your fucking head in, so a won't eh" Bob is raging "Bob, relax."

We put Harry in the car and take him to an old storage unit over Teesport, owned by one of our pals Paul Evo, Evo was discreet and owed Bob and me a favour, we collected a few quid for him he had tied up in some oil company, big figures. We chained Harry to a girder like in some old black and white Capone movie, in front of a bag of 'talking tools,' we need answers! "Who paid you" Bob is straight in like he's a punch bag, at this point I could just let Bob go crazy, we knew H didn't do it but we knew he knew who did, three hours passed and Bob gets the chainsaw, we brought this for effect a mean neither of us knew how to start the bastard thing, Harry gives up, spitting blood and teeth and unable to open his eyes he lets it out "it was Alex, fucking Alex, he wanted me in but I said no" Bob untied him and he dropped to the floor like a coat in a wardrobe, Bob mumbled into his ear, as he falls to the floor "you let me beat the shit out of you for hours to protect Alex the fucking hammer, why?". "Come on big man we're off" I tapped him on the arm, but before we left Harry, Bob turns and walks back towards him, then tells him "a wanna grand off ya", that was the cherry on top after all that Bob charged him a grand, the cheek of it but that's how Bob operates.

We have a name and we know that Alex drinks in some shithole over the border called the Steampacket, this place housed Teesside's infamous on most nights, it was an illegal shite hole, that sold illegal moonshineand that meant there were no rules, if they don't have rules, then neither do we. We would have many enemies in there, and without Frank, Chris and Norman we could be a target, Bob didn't give a fuck, someone tried to kill us two weeks ago and that was all he was thinking about.

By now everyone knew who we were looking for who and why, it was the talk of the town, which wasn't ideal. Bob and me would turn up everywhere and every door team would say the same thing before we opened our mouths, "he's not here lads, we haven't seen him" so we try the Steam packet, against my wishes, but this was Bob's call and that meant it was mine too, the owner of the dump called us, "lads look he's not here a swear it" Bob replies "be quiet we're on our way." The doorman see us pass and gives us a nervous nod, the owner is outside having a fag like it was his last and they're all having an internal hope that we aren't popping in. I park up and leap out of the motor, same story "he's not here lads" shouts the little one out of the two, Bob steps out and goes to the boot, pulling out two barrels in plain sight, we are not giving a fuck, Bob is holding her down one side of his leg as we approach the door, I am in front all you can hear is footsteps, the doorman sees what's going on "lads fucksake he's not here, and the boss is in tonight, Bob barked back at the fat doorman "the boss? Dicko? Tell fucking Dicko am coming back, a wanna grand off him for letting that little rat in here." He left an hour ago honest he's not here" holding his hands up palms showing like we were about to rob him, "well you won't mind us having a fucking quick look around then will ya, and tell the fucking boss al do a line off his nappa" Bob mumbles, "eh you what, fucking step aside" "alright alright Bob" whispers the big fella, Bob tucks two barrels under his coat and the pair step aside like we have leprosy, in we go and immediately attract attention, behind the bar we can just see the top of Dicko's head, crouched down keeping out the way, people looking away like they haven't seen us, we circle the place it's dark, dingy and unsafe, but we need to be seen in here and giving the odd shitbag a nod wouldn't do any harm, everyone who gets close says "alright lads" double checking their not on some shit list of ours, the place was full to the brim with people we have battled with over the years, from school right the way through to now, but adrenaline marched us both round the dump untouched, they knew the only bother we were looking for was with that little cunt Alex.In the corner the twins Richie and Johnny wearing their finest suits, draped in females, we have to acknowledge these two cunts so I give the nod, then Bob deliberately lets his jacket fall open and butt end of our girl takes a peek "oops" says Bob and re-adjusts himself saying fuckall, the twins just nod, war was not what they were about, the place stinks of betrayal and fear, there's no sign of Alex but plenty of his boys are out and one them is lingering, as we get ready to leave we are stopped at the door, "now then you two, who you looking for" it's Daz Robinson, this angers Bob, he never liked this scruffy bastard and he knew he was working for the hammer.

Bob slides two barrels out of his coat slowly and discreetly snuggles her nostrils under his fucking ginger stubble.Daz grows six inches, as the cold steel tickles his face, he looks like a ballerina on his tip toes, whilst Bob smiles with both sets of teeth showing, Bob has a fantastic way with the English language, "listen to me you scruffy ginger cunt, I will spread you off every fucking wall in this shit hole if you stop me again" this cunt dropped his drink and developed a bit of a stutter, Bob wanted to spread him like Nutella, I quickly followed it up with "you tell your mate Alex, we have been ok" "Jesus Christ" he cried, Bob tucks her away again and shoves this cunt to the floor, "let's go big man" I was feeling uneasy in here, before we walk away Bob turns to Daz, "a wanna grand off ya, for being a scruffy ginger cunt", seemed fair enough to me, "nice one fellas" I shout to the two lads standing there like we are fucking zombies, "yea catch ya later" they shouted but they never wanted to see us again if they're honest, the message was well and truly sent, half of the town seen that, just what we wanted. We knew by now that Alex, wherever he was, he would know what just happened, phones would be red hot, but that was the plan. Riding around the town with two barrels under the seat wasn't a clever move especially after what half of Teesside's blue giro collectors just witnessed and the reputation we had, so she had to go back to bed and fast the old bill knew there was tension in the town and they knew who with. Before we headed off home we made a quick stop off at the Bongo a local haunt for undesirables of the town, if there was a shitbag that could tell us something we would find it here.This place was like the bar in the film star wars and we were the Jedi.Now the old boy who worked the reception was a black guy with a bald head, he kept a shotgun under the desk, he was always wary of Bob and me since the night Bob smashed a can of red stripe off his nappa, you see Bob was doing a double bicep pose on the dance floor, being a general nuisance in his vest and this old boy walks over to put Bob straight.Well Bob thought he was Errol from Hot Chocolate and when he refused to sing you sexy thing for Bob there was hell on, a mean if Bob asks you to sing 'you sexy thing' you fucking sing.

That night the cunt pulled a shooter on me and Bob, so Bob took it off him and polished his head with a cloth and some pledge. We created an atmosphere, everywhere we went, and Errol wasn't happy that we put his place on edge but there wasn't anything in there for us, the same story from the doorman "he's not here lads", "Let's go Bob" it's getting risky.

The next week everyone was on alert.Social clubs and bars were becoming the whispering grounds for people to talk about who was going to do what and who would win, we stood in a bar minding our own business and some old boy started telling us about Bob and Dave, interesting story and not a single word of it true, "so who is this Bob and Dave you're talking about fella?" Bob teased the bloke, who replied. "Well these two are crazy, you don'twant to get mixed up with them, I feel sorry for that other bloke they're looking for" we both laughed, and Bob says, "you tell that fat bastard Bob or Dave that I am goanna punch fuck out of the both of them" this bloke thought we were mad, "I'm keeping out of it" he quickly stated. Anyway, we bought him a drink and were on our way. It was more than apparent that the whole place was talking about it, us, Harry, the attempt on our lives and Alex but we had to not get involved in the gossip.

The next morning we were woken by a thunderous knock on the door, I reached for the bat and peered through the window, it was the police half a dozen CID scattered across our lawn like weeds in the grass all staring up at the windows, I woke Bob and crept downstairs, "what do you want?" I shouted through an open letterbox, my voice all croaky half asleep, "open the door Dave, is Bob in there with you?" laughed some never seen before plod, "we just want a quick word it will take five minutes." I asked if they had a warrant and their reply was "just open the fucking door," that meant no.It felt ok, if they really wanted us the door would have been laying on the floor in pieces. I opened the door and a patient DS, enters at his own pace, he clocks the bat and laughs "now then you two love birds" Bob snaps back with "fuckoff dickhead and keep the noise down or you will wake your lass up" Bob points to the ceiling. "Harhar" he replied, the smile wiped off his face, maybe his lass never came home last night, that would have been funny. "Right al make this quick, I don't know what is going on around here but we had a complaint about two little crackpots running around scaring folk, any ideas?" Both Bob and me have perfected the art of looking dumb at each other like we can't even understand his language never mind what he's saying. Me being the rational one I piped up first "nah we were in all night never moved off the sofa, ain't that right Bob? Why what happened?" This fella didn't buy a single word of it, "look cut the shit, some of us aren't sure if it were you two, some are, we know there is shit going down, we know you have trouble with that idiot Alex, we also know Harry Brown is in a bad way on ward 4, he fell over apparently, be warned," then they left but before they left Bob shouted him back, and mumbles "a wanna grand off ya" then realises it's the old bill and bursts out laughing, Bob just can't help himself. "Just fuckoff" he replied, no sense of humour these cunts, but they knew more than we did, then that's Teesside for you, some payroll shitbag already on the blower dropping names.

Things were becoming on top, Frank, Chris, and Norm were all out of the way down south because of some murder and we had a job to get on with, so the plan was to let the hot water cool, well that was my plan but Bob had another idea, "let's get this Bastard while the iron is hot," I needed a quick response. "More heat Bob, they're already onto us." "He tried to kill us bro" Bob was right for the first time ever he was right.

For the next week it was re-group, think and decide our next move remembering the filth were all over us this wasn't going away, old bill following us around town, the gym, they even followed us to the shithouse, we would take them on a ride just for the crack but it was becoming tedious, they knew our every move, Alex the hammer had to go on the back burner his time would come.

Ace of hearts...

Back to work and we hadn't been the gym for two days which was a poor show the City of Steel was our home through the day.Undercover old bill training looking to befriend Bob an me in the bag room, brand new gym wear, new bags, new brains, not a clue how to put their wraps on, Bob looked pissed off and mutters "do we look fucking dumb?" "Alright lads how long you been training in here?" A brave undercover plod mutters to Bob. Bob is fed up of these fuckers trying to infiltrate our shit, "we fucking live here ya daft pair of cunts, now if you interrupt me once more al smash ya lass ya daft cunt, Mike Delta Lima, al punch fuck outta ya" I burst out laughing and gave some advice to these two idiots "best fuckoff and set up ya speed camera lads." Bob follows up with "go on fuckoff" and like ants evading a child with a magnifying glass they were gone. "A swear down Dave al smash his lass" Bob repeated himself. "Bob you don't know his lass, he was old bill" I just thought I would drop that to him. Bob was always fairly sharp with his response, "a don't give a fuck al find her!" "Alright mate let's just train we're working tonight."A lot of the time I still had a look of disbelief on my face with this cunt. Bob's mind was always on the tax, always thinking, wanting war, we had a tip off that some lowlifes were meeting to play a high stakes poker game in a warehouse owned by our very own pal MrBoo, now Boo was a serious businessman, a big deal in the property world, the cash we collected for him run into hundreds of thousands, we were really good friends of his and this tip off was worth five grand all day long, this was right up our street and it was to happen whilst we were at work which meant it was perfect. Bob was keen, this was his job and a fucking flawless plan was needed.

In our club there was a cellar, that run the length of the street and out through and old disused beer keg entrance, the cellar was huge, infect there was a fully made up bed with clean sheets, that one of the lads took pride in keeping right for his female encounters during the shift.I fucking shit you not.

The plan was simple and it was Bob's, we go to work, white shirts and throw our weight about, to get noticed, slip out of the club via the cellar past the fucking doorman's bedroom, get changed, into something more suitable and hit this fucking poxy card game, get back the same way we left, white shirts on, back to work before the scaffs arrive for their monthly night out, had to be before the scaffs arrive because some of Teesside's scaff crew were how do you say it, naughty fish, and naughty fish can validate our presence. "fucking brilliant Bob" I agreed, this was perfect a mean we would need Sean involved, but he was cool and would need to cover us.

Everything is in place, we turn up for work and Bob is slapping folk already, "get back inside with that drink ya daft cunt, or al smash ya lass" Bob was on form tonight, taking a grand off everyone who kicks off, he says it's to make sure people know we are at work, I say it's because he is a fucking nutter but there was a theory I guess. At this poker game there was some big players, the towns so called old school elite and a possible fifty grand pot that was already Bob's, so local plod engage in conversation on the front door and this is perfect, who knows who these plod are connected to, if you get me. Bob and me make it our business to chat shit to the uniform nightshift, "yea goanna be a long night here fella" Bob shouts with a fake laugh, "don't overdo it mate" time to go it's midnight and we suggest that we go inside, "ok lads" agrees Sean with a quick nod, in we go, the disappearance into the cellar is slick, like magicians we vanished, one at a time we're gone we pass the bedroom that's spotless, we get changed hanging up our white shirts and ties on coat hangers, we grab trusty two barrels, she's never let us down, after we exit the cellar in an abandoned street, put on our fake padlock on the keg door, and into a car driven by a friend of Franks, we have about forty five minutes before questions would be asked, the club was choker block on with the job. "Let's get in smash fuck out of every cunt in there before we take our cash" whispers Bob, "no Bob, we get in there and take the cash and leave, ok yea?" I replied.I needed this cunt to agree but he never agreed to anything sensible. Pulling into the yard next to the small warehouse, we could see activity this game was nearly over so we needed to be quick, in through the back door ballys down, remembering that this lot were all fucking criminals of the highest order, now there were some supreme shitbags sat at this table, bigwigs and high rollers none of which have spent much time on the other side of the big fence oddly enough, so its best I take charge of two barrels as well as do the talking.

In we go as calm as you like and I shout nice and clear like a Sergeant major in my best scouse, "gentleman and daft cunts, keep your hands on the table, this won't take a minute we are not interested in your shite pathetic lives," then someone at the table decides to mumble "your fucking kidding me?" Bob slaps the fucking snot out of him, there is too much twitching going on, boom I let the celling have it, and everycunt freezes. "Do you know who we are?" shouts some old boy, who was clearly expecting an answer. Bob hates nothing more than to be 'do you know who Iam'd, he puts the cash down and uppercuts this silly cunt for about a week, after collecting the poke from this bunch of 'how dare you rob us old farts', we back off to the exit slowly, I am scanning the place sweeping left to right, this could become a saloon mess in an instant, they are probably carrying, we padlock the door to buy us time, outside the car awaits, boom I let our old girl breath once more, we knew that if any of these cunts thought it was Bob and me all hell would break loose, we needed to get back to the club and be seen. Within 15 minutes we were back to the club, in the cellar cash and two barrels were put to sleep, shirts on and eased back into the club like the fucking draught, "let's get back on the front door Bob, we need to be seen." My heart rate was through the roof, making eye contact with Sean was a relief, we're back at it like nothing happened being polite to customers and Bob chucking his usual threats out, "get back inside with that drink al punch your fucking head in" ten minutes later a car pulls up, out jumps three of the card players and they're walking over to the club. "Gents" Sean greets them but they aren't here for a drink they're here to see if Bob and me are here and to theirdisappointment there we are, standing as clean as a whistle, like fucking guardsman at BuckinghamPalace, they're fucking raging. "Alright lads?" shouts Bob, "sound yea" mutters one of them, now these fuckers were scratching their heads and only Bob, me and Sean knew why. They were convinced we just robbed these bastards now they're back to the drawing board.

This one went down in the history books of Teesside's biggest mysteries, gangsters turning on each other for information.Later that week we were even offered money, to see if we could find out any information about what had happened and by who, fucking muppets. So, we paid Sean well and sent a very large sum of cash to Scotland and never stopped laughing at these daft cunts who were still scratching their heads.Even the old bill knew about this game of cards.Carta invited us into the police station for an informal chat, which we politely told him to fuck off I mean come on, Carta wasn't stitching us again.

So, the property game was booming and we took over the door scene completely in the town, if the place has a fucking door we looked after it, we had every bar from

Northallerton right through Teesside and Stockton, bashing our way to the top, fighting like we were swimming with the salmon.We would troubleshoot on wherever the bother was happening at the time.

One night we got a call from one of our bar's in town, half a dozen doorman from Durham have decided to have a night out in the boro, which is fine as long as they have manners, as this meant they had to show some respect in our homeland, but this bunch of Pit village monkeys were showing no respect in Bob and Dave's gaff and that is never a good move.We pick up Sean and pop round to see what's what, now normally we like to wait til everyone is outside and in true Teesside fashion, bouncing around like a shite boxer with no top on, so you could see that he had done his traps that day, belcher chain swinging with a moll girlfriend begging him not to "hurt you", we usually have a giggle at this spectacular mutant performance, because that's all it ever really was a performance, but these guys were your typical stereotypes. I mean am talking bald heads, DM's and all wearing their bomber jackets, "fuck sake man I want to go get some grub" "we got to go see Baz remember""do we have to?" I moaned. Bob's reply was predictable really "yes we fucking do," I count six dickheads, Sean pointed out that at least two of them shouldn't even be doormen so that leaves four, there were three of us and we were used to taking two a piece, the maths was done and these idiots were already in trouble, in goes Sean, you see he's the diplomat he has a way with words and has the ability to offer them a way out peacefully. Bob was already in there right behind them at the bar, completely unseen, I was to be their focus, I mean this was child's play we have done this routine hundreds of times it was like a performance, they weren't drunk so that makes this situation a little more disrespectful, now there is always a leader or head doorman so it's important to take him first. So the scene is set and all we need is someone to shout, act 1 scene 1 fucking action. Sean enters the arena with his palms showing and a calm adult tone, I give him ten seconds then I come into the bar like the wind, "fellas make this your last drink we're closing" shouts Sean above the music and verbal shite these cunts were talking, then the brave one, there is always a brave one, with a stupid look on his face yells "you're not Bob or Dave" Sean was as sharp as a Japanese blade, and replies with "yea that's right am not, I'm black magic" well Bob spits his drink out laughing all over them from a quiet spot behind, I laugh out loud because Bob spat his drink and Sean who thought his black magic line was uber James Bond, remained rather serious. Sean was particular about his humour, most didn't get him because he was intellectually challenging, but I did, the whole thing was a bit of a carry on with the doorman.

Bob was into collecting teeth, human teeth of gobshites that fucked about on the patch, so in an instant, as planned it was all over and as they were piled up on the pavement one after another like bin bags on a Wednesday after Boxing Day we had to nash. Bob took a grand off them for our time, Bob always took a grand off people who caused shit, they finally got to meet this 'Bob and Dave' only sadly they wouldn't remember, so we got out of there and took the CCTV footage with us.

The portfolio...

Next stop we needed to go and see an old pal 'big Baz Zimmer' now Baz was a quiet nutter our business paths never usually crossed, he respected us and we returned the favour, Baz was having a little bother with his girls, now he had a very profitable thing going on in Teesside with the ladies of the night, now am not talking about the toothless dinner ladies that wear their knickers inside out after day four and that poison the pavement with their scruffy buns and boyfriends. Baz's girls are next level you need to know Baz to know his girls, these girls all know their way around the Dragonara hotel. We meet Baz and half a dozen of his beauties in a nice part of town, "alright Baz, ladies?" Both me and Bob mutter at the same time, "lads come in, come in grab a seat" Baz is all over us like the draught. Which meant the cunt needed us, a mean this cunt wasn't our bag, even though he was a naughty boy and if he needed us that meant cash, the cunt was loaded, a modern day pimp, only without the purple velvet suit, hat trimmed with leopard skin and walking cane.We never drink on business meetings but big Baz was sipping champagne like water, well we are having some of that. "So, what's up Baz, what do you need us for" I lock into the job, because this cunt wasn't our thing, so basically his girls are getting a rough time with their wealthy punters and this has to stop, also Baz needs a place for them to make their money, his place got turned over, so Bob is straight onto this. "Right Baz, let's not fuck about here, we have ten houses standing empty, good houses and the girls, you give them our number and we will meet their punters and have a word beforehand, how's that? We'll treat these girls like our own and al punch fuck out of anyone that upsets them ok?" "Fuck me Dave he's on the ball" "Yea can't get nowt past Bob Baz." Baz likes the deal and he knows it's gonna cost him. During the meeting one of the girls was being picked up by a limo, so me and Bob demonstrated the service we were offering Baz, up pulls the stretched motor and Cassandra links the arms of Bob and me, we walk out to the car and Bob opens the door, sat in the back is some suit, the motor stinks of cash and Bob helps our new princess into the back then crouches down to his level. "Now then, I'm Bob and this is my man Dave, you take good care of her yea?" Bob can do passive-aggressive when he wants to.This guy suddenly pinned back his ears, "yea no problem lads am just here for a good night, no trouble yea?" I follow up with "Cassy you call me babe" and they were off, job done. Baz was happy but this cunt was red hot the law was all over him so business wasn't to mix with pleasure on this occasion.We talked some figures and shook hands adding Teesside's ladies to our portfolio, a mean Bob loved the title 'pimp' but I wasn't keen.

Things were coming together, we worked our way through the town like Pac-Man in the maze of cash and opportunities.Our sense of entitlement was growing, on the occasion we used a taxi driver they would say "Mr Bob it's no problem" to whichBob would reply "fucking right it's no problem ya daft cunt al punch ya fucking head in" and I would have to shove the cunt out the cab.

We had a considerable amount of tax free cash up in Scotland at this stage and we wanted to make it work for us, we had fingers in most pies, clubs, pubs, girls, taxes, you name it.We needed something a little more legit.So,Bob thought that we could run head first into the food game and sothe Parmo was born.

Bob had a great idea that I thought was a little brash, he halted production and the sale of the so called Parmo in every fucking Boro restaurant, it was a new dish the town was going mad for, now if Bob wants something he wants it, he wanted to be the founder, this made sense. We walked into each restaurant who sold it, asked for the owner and a meeting, everyone says yes, we politely told them over a coffee the same thing "listen you fucking mug stop selling the Parmo in here for a month, ya daft cunt or al punch fuck out of every single one of ya, including your staff and their mams, don't worry al let you put it back on the menu soon." After five seconds of negotiation and jaws picked up off the floors in disbelief our demands were met, so the infamous Parmo disappeared.

People were in uproar, restaurants denied selling it, but so fuck, we re-launched it in our new restaurant that we named the Europa, this place had just opened and was struggling, so we offered him a silent cash injection in the form of an offer he didn't fucking dare refuse and a new dish that Bob called 'the parmo.'He was a nice bloke and agreed to sell the main course delight that you all love to this very day, naturally we used our charm and business acronym to seal the deal. So, whatever you have heard across Teesside about where the dish was first created you now know, the Parmo belongs to us and sixty percent of the restaurant was in our hands, all we needed to do was eat in there once in a while, to show face.

Now, wherever we went old bill were never too far behind us even to entertain their wives they would visit the Europa. Invites for a 'chat' were regularly met with "al tell yaworrit is ya daft cunt ya better fuck off," and me pulling Bob away from the unmarked shitbag that kerb crawls us was quite common practice late at night, sometimes I did the talking after putting Bob in the car and fastening his seatbelt like a naughty kid who's doing his Mams head in.My approach would be a lot more sympathetic, "look lads I know you have a job to do but you wanna quit upsetting the big man like that, I can't always hold him back" with a grin on my face, "Ere Dave we hear you and Baz are pals now, ooh he's a wrong un that one, he's not in your league" and he laughs thinking this was some sort of banter.

Now, I always made it my business to find out the name of a bent coppers wife, I knew that many because they were all fucking bent, remembering them was tricky if I got it right it killed the conversation, so I could always walk away ontop I would quickly reply "no wonder Linda fucks about" and am gone, "cheeky cunt" was usually his next move, imagine though if Linda was fucking about, the damage that would do, these cunts are wasting their time talking to Bob and me they were better off meeting the blue giro lot in a country pub for a 'bite to eat', but they knew this already it was more to try and wind us up to be fair.

So our nights were becoming busy, clubs, girls, restaurants, property and there was our out of town work, that really pulled in the poke, Bob and me were busy little bees, it was rare that we had to sort out any mess for Baz and his girls but trouble was always going to surface.

We gets a distress call from one of the girls Tekeesha, she was in one of our houses having difficulty with some wanker in a suit, she phones me on the sly crying down the phone, "right ok sweetheart we're on our way, stop crying hunny it's going to be ok just keep him there" well Bob was listening in to the call and was salivating, "cheeky cunt in

161

our house, turning over one of our girls" Bob is amazed at the balls some people have, we pull up and Bob is in the boot gloves on he's round the back of the house.

I let myself in and on the sofa is Tekeeaha sobbing, she points into the kitchen and I bring my finger to my lips "shhh" I mime"it's ok" and usher her out the house silently to go wait in the car, this was all done with seal team precision. I'm now in the living room and the punter is in the kitchen, with Bob at the back door key in the lock, this cunt walks in and drops everything he was holding making a mess of our floor. Bob's cue to enter and he enters like a pit bull in a dogfight, dragging this cunt out the back to the fish pond in his boxer shorts in between a smack in the mouth and a dunk in the pond we hand this guy some manors "you got something you wanna say boy?" Bob repeated several times, his babbles and gurgles didn't make much sense so we took him to Tekeesha who was still shaken, "am really sorry, am really sorry" he spurts, "right here's the deal, you pay her, then you apologise to Baz, when Baz lets me know you have done this, I want a grand off ya, otherwise al punch your fucking head in" Bob put down the deal, it was one sided and not up for negotiation, "ok okok" Bob threw him to the pavement like a cheap tracksuit from Manchester and we got off.Tekeesha was safely dropped off with Baz.We had Baz in our pocket, but he loved it, the old man kicked our names about like a football in Parkend, no wonder the old bill knew about our relationship.We never spent any time with old Baz, just to collect our poke so we were safe.

We never sat still, Wednesday right through to Monday we would pop up here and there making appearances, I could see that Bob was still twisting over Alex, he was never going to let it go until something was sorted. I thought it was best we took a little break to Spain to get him out of the way before we accidentally bumped into Alex on doggy market, then all hell would break loose in broad daylight. Bob agreed and he loved a hot country, "yea fucking right a want to go away let's get out of this dump!" So, we tie up loose ends, The Sarge would take care of Baz and his business if needed, the restaurant was doing ok, and the doors were all covered, I made a call to my pal Curtis and he let us have his villa for a while, we were to leave for Spain in a week.

Alex is found...

As we prepare for our break, it's the gyma good diet and this holiday is what we need. Bob needs a distraction away from going crazy over that little cunt who tried to end our world, so we make some last minute calls.I liked everything going smooth, no fuckups.We packed our bags, I could see that the thought of being away on holiday was helping Bob and calming him down, we were both in a good place.

Friday night, our last shift before we fly Saturday morning, business as usual Bob slapping wannabes and draping the ladies over his arms like an expensive fur. Bob could be a ladies man when he wanted to be, we had cash to throw around and he would often entertain half a dozen girls in a roped off area with champagne just for the craic. Bob would be telling jokes only he laughed at, well everyone laughed, not because he was funny but if you didn't, you may get your fucking head punched in.

Now, I wanted a nice quiet, easy shift but it was anything but, females looking for 'our lad' kicking off outside because 'our lad' has been out all day. The wives and girlfriends can be as dangerous as the fellas, they carry their boyfriends status around town like a badge, so if he sells the powder then she is on it and all her friends are too, usually for free, believe me there will be a lot of them, free dust is like rice falling off the back of a lorry in Africa in Teesside and that means if he sells the dust then he's a tough guy and he says she can do what she likes, which is very decent of him. Bob hated these wenches they're awful and have not a single ounce of class or respect, their Teesside accent breaks the fucking glass and poisons the air like fag smoke, every sentence starts with "ere" and ends with "fuuuuckoffff," they're usually well-dressed because money is no object, their faces are frozen, the Daffy Duck lips haven't kissed a human being in years in fear of an explosion, their hair like wood shavings freshly planed of the door and make-up that takes half a day to render on the face and lasts for a year because it was plastered on in some other wenches kitchen who calls herself, 'Make-up by Makala' or some other shite name, their whole getting ready process takes all day and transforms them into a fraudulent version of what they see on television, they never go out with their bloke but always meet up when there pissed and want an argument about that slag he got caught shagging a hundred years ago, this usually happens in one of our places, where she is outside holding her high heels in her hands because her feet are rotten with blisters, the 'Make-up by Makala' now looks like make-up by the six year old daughter and the outfit that will soon be abandoned in the wardrobe with all the other worn once items of shite, is struggling to hold its value. This coked up pile of shit and her pals are now outside wanting trouble with their respective partners, because he's inside and so is the slut that he is still side piecing, "get him out ere" gets repeated over and over until we get fed up and ask the law to intervene.

Now, he is on point, he isn't even drunk, he's a tough guy remember he has a reputation to keep and a side piece to impress, while she staggers from side to side telling the crowd outside about his infidelity and their 'kids at home', whilst he's inside ignoring the fact she is his baby Mama. This is a Teesside tradition handed down through generations of undesirable shite, father to son, as important as the first pint, it's as popular as Bob and Dave'sParmo, as common as the tikka marsala on Boro Road, it happens week in week out and half the time Bob and me spend half the night defending these fuckers, "look babe he's not even here, just get yourself home" I am quite polite at first and the low life with the side piece who's slipping Bob a purple back to get rid of her patiently waits inside, make no mistake a Teesside moll that is drunk, perturbed, angry and is holding her heels can take your eye out in no time at all and she fucking will.These mutant girls get the same treatment as their fellas, so when this girl swings her heels at the doorman she needs to go to kip as quickly as possible, it's the only way.In slow motion I can see her dipping into the depths of her tobacco stained lungs to gather a phlegm ball for my face, before it left her mouth she was knocking out zeds, after sliding down the shutter I even gave her a pillow and the partner, well he was too busy with the side piece. Our night before the holiday was never going to be an easy shift they were all in, scaffs, riggers, molls, merc driving whiff droppers and strangely Teesside's finest, I mean there was more deep voice in here than on ten platforms, it was testosterone wars because when this lot get together it's about the aesthetics, tight tops freshly sprayed on, the more boisterous you can be the better man you are, a mean these fuckers are breaking all the rules, taking drinks outside, slapping people for no reason, we need a handle on this fast, felt like there was something in the airand people were whispering the name 'Alex' in conversations over cigarettes, Bob was not happy that he was hearing his name.At that a Mercedes slowly drives past our club, the windows were tinted and half rolled down, like a movie scene, a man sits forward, glances then disappears, "is that Alex" I whispered to Bob "eh you what, al fucking kill that cunt" rages Bob, "easy big man they have gone" I wasn't even sure if it was him, it probably wasn't but what it did was tell me how much we needed to get away, also plenty of people heard Bob shout, including the beat bobby that was passing, all I needed was Bob calm, we go on holiday tomorrow get inside with me let's grab a drink.

Then at closing time when the scaffs would begin their forage, for the eternal party, that ends up in some cunts kitchen all night, with row upon row of dust that isn't paid for, on a kitchen work surface that they prep food for the children's packed lunches and the mobile phones all prepared, each one with a different scum bag to contact, all set to send that text to the low life when the supplies are low, for that all important drop off by the Columbian postman. In these places they talk more shit than parliament, they talk of fights, wallpaper, patio doors, MMA and boxing whilst disputing which one is best, they talk of the love they have for each other, there will be hugs and kisses and plenty of "I love you kidda" with shite music playing a little too loud in the background as they relive that fucked up holiday in Ibiza last year where 'one of the lads' overdosed and it was all funny as fuck, or maybe not, there are only two things in the world that stops this crescendo, three if you include Bob and Dave turning up to tax the life out the powder, one is daylight and the other is no response from the usually punctual and overpriced lowlife who is paid to turn up in a taxi at any point in the night. The next hurdle these boys are waiting for is the social club to open, so they stick it out, the shit talk is flowing and so is the dust. As the sun pierces the window like a laser and the scaffs battle on, whilst we do the rounds before getting back home and ready for our holiday. The texts awaken Bob and me one after the other, beep beep, beep beep, all saying the same message, a thousand all night party's across Teesside wanting to send the same message, the tone of the kitchen disco turns, Bob wakes like a bear that's been disturbed from hibernation, "what the fuck is this shit, my phone has been going all morning, fucking fuming al punch fuck out of every single one of them" he grunts bumbling downstairs in his apple catchers. I am already up, coffee is made "Bob, I have been getting the same messages bro, have you read them?" I asked him because I guessed he hadn't, "can't be arsed kid what's going on?" he mutters scratching his balls, "Police have found a body and everyone is saying it's Alex" Bob is straight on it checking his phone, "yea same messages bro, fucking get in there" Bob was over the moon but pissed off as well, if this was even true, we never got to sort our business out.

Whilst Bob fluctuated from fuming to happiness I was saying, "Bob we need to get out of here, they're gonna blame us, they will be here as soon as they identify this body," "but we didn't touch the cunt Dave, if he's dead am gonna punch fuck out of him" part of that made sense, but would this stop us being lifted four hours before our flight, not a fucking chance.

We have to leave...

Right now I need to think, I take over this situation, "Bob grab your case, get ready we leave in 20 mins" I ordered Bob upstairs and for the first time he did it without a threat, we didn't reply to any of the messages, pointless fuelling the fire. Suitcase packed and in the car we're off, "ere we didn't do it, al punch that cunt out if he's alive" Bob is raging we didn't know what was what, but what I knew was that they were gonna come and get us, I sent messages to Chris and Frank to find out what the details are, nothing, just that they have found a body, male 24 years old and he's been punched fucked an out of, "the whole fucking town thinks we did it, even the law thinks we did."

Now, Bob was gonna punch this cunt out alive or dead, but I knew this was not good for us, at the airport I am on full alert, nobody knows that we're going away "Bob we need to get the fuck out of here" I had to remind the big daft cunt he was still buzzing about this dead bloke, and the only info we were getting was from the zombie scaffs who are probably standing on their own doorsteps attempting to sweet talk the girlfriend round to actually letting them in from the all-nighter she knew nothing about. We phoned Frank and Chris, they knew it wasn't us straight away but feared the same as I did, that the law might get Bob and me off the streets once and for all. Bob just wanted to punch fuck out of everything that breathed, "lay low in the airport Bob, we need to get on this fucking flight" pulling him into the departure lounge wearing geggs and looking like something out of midnight express, I grab a magazine from the shop, then I hear out loud "eh al punch ya fucking head in ya mug" Bob is at the till being short changed by a man that looks like Jimmy Saville, a mean this is all we need, "oi fuck sake, move it" for once in my life I gripped him like a parent that has pulled him away from the sweetieaisle. Bob needed to take a piss and a chill.He's been in there ten minutes, fuck sake I go in, all I can here is Bob "al punch your fucking head in", he has some little shit bag off the floor and pinned to the wall "what the fuck?" I yelled at him I mean the amazement has now left the building, "what are you doing Bob?" Bob fires back, "this cunt owes me fifty quid" he was choking some guy from Teesside that he had been looking for since nursery school, we have now attracted more attention to our ourselves than a copper having a line, this is all we need some little gobshite telling Teesside, Bob and Dave were on their way to Spain.

Its half ten in the morning and Teesside's weekend Columbians are still awake waiting for the offy to open, or the social club their noses are inoperative, still sending messages asking the crack and wanting confirmation from Bob and me. We aren't in the clear until we're leaving the airport and have arrived on the other side and this seemed like a lifetime away.

Boarding the plane we need to be discreet, Bob sticks his head in the cockpit, "listen, get us in the air you two pair of daft cunts, or al punch fuck out of ya, eh, ere a wanna grand off ya, and get one of these birds to bring us some grub" now he said this with a slight hint of humour and even let out a little laugh but there was also a shit load of 'am being serious.'The captain laughed as Bob was coaxed to his seat, each moment that passes I am amazed that this cunt hasn't had us locked up for just being fucking alive. Touching down on the other side and walking through the airport with Spanish security all wearing dark glasses, not knowing if their eyes were on us, or whether they didn't give a shit about the ten ton of British pissheads that had just landed on their mother soil and are already spilling onto the floor, all ready to blow every penny they brought with them on shite booze whilst giving headaches out like sweets.

We get the nod and our pal Curtis has sent a driver to collect us, we're off, this big daft cunt is in full holiday mode but I am worried the old bill will make something of our coincidental departure from Teesside, it's just a good thing we have our own place so we can keep our heads down. Bob is meeting the locals "al punch your fucking head eh you what" shaking my head from side to side in total disbelief that our low key arrival was being thwarted by this Teesside monster in the local shop over a Solero and ten pesetas, our heads down were anything but down.

Back home the details started to surface about the body that was found, it was Alex H 'The Hammer' the papers described him as "a menace to Teesside, a prolific drugs baron and a violent individual, with plenty of enemies" he was apparently punched fuck out of and his head had been punched in, you can see why we were panicking there's only one man in Teesside that could and would cause injuries like that, only one man punches heads in, 'Bob.' Our phones were red hot.Newspapers reported that police wanted to speak to two local men aged 25 in connection with the murder, "I fucking knew it, what did I tell you these cunts want us off the streets well it's not happening." I was pacing the room, by now probably all 50 of our houses were being turned over, the fact that we hadn't come forward after a police appeal was making us look guilty. Teesside doors were being unhinged, restaurants raided, whore houses infiltrated, nightclubs swamped and blue giros getting printed faster than the green ones. Bigwigs selling info on Bob and Dave, these cunts had us found guilty and already sentenced before our fucking tan had even begun.

So the fight had started for the top job, Teesside's scramble to take it on now we're out the way, they're assuming we are about to lose control of the town, our faces now printed on the local shite paper as people of interest, to be 'eliminated from enquires' yea right fuck off, but I guess the longer we were out of Teesside the more we looked guilty, we were in a no win situation. Bob was right we didn't do it but we needed a plan, and not a Bob plan, we were not on holiday anymore, this was anything but.

"HOW WOULD I LIKE TO BE REMEMBERED? JUST A GOOD BLOKE. JUST A GOOD BLOODY BLOKE WHO LIKED A BIT OF TORTURE!"

BOB

10

The Final Stand

Things are murky and Spain is no holiday, our friend Curtis has arrived to check we're ok. Curtis is someone you should know if you're in trouble, he's got more connections than BT and if you bash fuck out of three men in jail that are about to kill him stone dead, then he is in your debt for life.This bloke is a millionaire and a menace to the law, has smuggled more goods across the world than Isaac Gulliver, he's been inside for everything you can imagine including manslaughter, Bob and me looked after him for six months whilst he was awaiting trial, he used to call us 'the sons he never had.' He was following the story on Teesside from his pad and wanted to make sure we were holding it together, he gave us a hug and reassured us that things would work out, advice from him was like a doctor giving a diagnosis, if we needed a lawyer he would sort it, he agreed with me that this was a shit storm and we needed a clear plan. Now Curtis was over on business, the kind we didn't want to get involved in so he didn't hang around but he left us some good advice, a shit load of cash and a promise to be there if we needed him, so for a few weeks we soaked up the sun.We didn't have a great time but we were in fucking Spain, mooching about the place was uneasy, Bob thought he spotted plod from the uk several times so we decided to grab supplies and stay indoors.Our villa was a fortress, so going to bed at night was easy we would have a few drinks around the pool and the big man usually cooked up a barbecue for two, always ended with us chatting shit. "when we get home am gonna punch fuck out of every cunt" Bob was showing his frustration because the heat back home was hotter than ever. "Bob when we get back they're gonna lock us up kid." I needed to remind him and keep things real. "So let's get our game on and heads straight." I was trying to reassure this big cunt but failing, so we turned in for the night. Laid in bed it's twenty five degrees, all I could hear was Bob snoring and the sound of Spanish crickets, making more noise than a primary school in Grove hill, full of Teesside's mini shitbags. There is no sleep in me it's like I have been spiked with the pinkest of champagne, the only light I see is the pool lights flickering off the water, all I can do is think and even that is cloudy, I keep telling myself we didn't do it so they can't pin it on us. Bob's snoring is waking up the next island, but who's going to tell him, there's only me on the planet that could get away with that so I get up to kick the cunt, the cold tiles on the floor are a comfort as I walk through the villa wearing nothing but my shreddies.

I shimmy into Bob's cave he's flat out lifting the roof off, "Bob fucksake ya big cunt," I shouted in a whisper as I kick him he stops breathing for about nine month, then continues, it's then I hear something, I freeze, pointing my ear in the direction of where it come from, waiting, there it is again "what the fuck?" I whisper to myself because Bob is still in the land of the dead, I wasn't imagining it, something isn't right, the blinds flicker, the open patio door breathes gently. I leave Bob sleeping and tiptoe through the place picking up a bat along the way like I was in a supermarket, I hear it again a rustle, I back myself up into Bob's room, he's talking in his sleep "al smash ya lass ya daft cunt eh you what" "Bob, Bob, Bob wake up" I poked him with the bat, the bear wakens and is startled, "eh what's up what the fuck, who me, al smash ya lass ya mug, fuckoff" he mumbles shite half asleep, "look lively, somethings not right here" I was sharper now and so was Bob now that his brain has engaged, he leaps out of his pit and throws his tracksuit on, "shhh, listen" we are both on full alert, holding a bat each and moving around the pad slowly, if some cunt is breaking into Curtis's pad and is greeted by Bob and me they're in the shit big time. "It's coming from out near the pool," mutters Bob in an almost silent whisper, it's not Curtis because he would have phoned, "al punch fuck out of any cunt that comes near us Dave" Bob is ready to swing this fucker like a pro, we edge towards the patio door, I peek through the blinds, I see silhouettes moving fast around the pool, "Bob we have company" I whispered, my heart is pounding Bob is like a New York Yankee ready to swing, the place is silent out of nowhere red dots appear on Bobs chest, six or seven, then onto my chest, "Bob,Bob don't even think about it" I shout to him, "Fuck, easy Bob" if anyone was goanna blow it was him, boom then there was an almighty crash, in goes the front door, we turn and the place is full of Spanish swat dressed head to toe in armour screaming in their shit language, "Ponte en el suelo" they're shouting over and over "Bob shouts ere ya daft cunts al punch fuck out every single one of ya" bang, he's struck in the stomach with the butt of a rifle, down he goes winded, I can't help him even though I want to it's my turn I'm dropped like a Teesside girls pants on a Saturday night, they're shouting shit at us in their fucked up tongue, me and Bob are face down out of breath and struggling to chuck out the threats.After what seems like a lifetime we're stood up on our feet helpless. Bob needs to say something, he gives no fucks, "a don't give a fuck who you are, al find ya al swim back over here and punch your fucking head in" then out of nowhere a Teesside accent walks into to the pad, "now then you two, now how the fuck have ended up in this place? Are you and Curtis pals? Tut tut, we need a word back on home soil." "Fuckoff you prick" Bob lunges forward, he couldn't help himself and we both get another drop to the floor.

We're bundled into a van like cheap meat in a slaughterhouse and driven to some Spanish shithole to be processed for transportation back to the UK.We felt like immigrants the whole time these pigs kicking and punching fuck out of us in the back of the van. The next morning these bastards released us to the British authorities. "You know the quicker you two admit what happened the easier it will be" this plod laughed. "Are you for real ya daft cunt, al snap ya fucking.." "Bob", I stopped him sharply, can't have him threatening these wankers. The next trip was being escorted back to Teesside, out of the nick with blankets over our head we were fucking fuming, treat like nonces we're raging.

On the way back it was a tug of war, Bob telling them to fuckoff, plod asking questionsand me, well I was thinking about the mess we were in.

Back in the nick we were processed rapidly, given shit food and the onslaught began.Local news reports were that two men were arrested in Spain in connection with the murder of that fucking little cunt Alex 'The Hammer,' there was only one short term outcome here, the big fence again until we were cleared.

We needed that hotshot lawyer from our man, a local solicitor from Teesside couldn't win a raffle they simply wouldn't cut it here, hours had passed and the odd faceless copper shouting "got you now" through the half open flap to wind us up was getting tedious. Shit sandwiches and cold tea begrudgingly skid through the hatch, like they were feeding an animal at the zoo, wasn't ideal, then true to his word, Curtis you beauty, in walked Mr Rupert Brampton-Russel.This pinstripe wearing slick beanpole was our saviour, his hair was like a fine rug with waves from Hawaii, he spoke with a mouth full of marbleshis plan was to inject us with a quick shot of confidence as soon as we met.He was flanked by two dolly birds ready to wipe his arse or brow should one require, each person he spoke to in the police station that wasn't involved in the defence, would receive the contemptuous tone that you could only learn over a thousand years in the Barr.

He had flown in from the big smoke on Curtis's orders, we knew we were going away but our man wanted to make a presence in the court, he was a well-known QC and was our legal fist to punch fuck out of every cunt involved in this.

Our stories always matched because it was the truth, we left the club at 2:00am, arrived at our restaurant the Europa for some food around 2:10am we left there and got home for 3:00am we even had CCTV footage off our cameras at home, which have gone missing. The problem was the time of death was between 2:00am and 6:00am.

We were to be charged and flanked by a dozen overweight courtroom fat bastard sheriffs, we were hauled up before some judgemental, school teacher magistrate who looked like he hated us from birth, but he didn't know our story or how we arrived on this planet, peering over his half-moon glasses as he drops his head in a bias disgust, like a disappointedGrandad who we have let down by not watering his cabbages up the allotment. I remember looking at Bob and us both shaking our heads, this is where the fight begins, this is where we have to take on the world but this time we would be doing it alone, this was the only fight we would be getting on with without each other, a fight we weren't allowed to do together, it was new territory and it somehow didn't feel right. Bob's brave face appeared and only I knew when this big bastard brought out the mask that was never seen, my big pal was worried.In this moment I was transported back to that time on the beach when we first met and I knew he was going to be my bro and growing up the difficulties we faced with our big people and the shit bags that took years to tame, the scraps we got ourselves into and the black eyes we would compare and laugh at and the lies we spun to protect each other, the close calls we encountered on a daily basis. In my daydream, which felt like an hour, I re-played every day like a projector in my mind, Bob is a hard case and fearless but he was just my big pal, someone only I could swear at, I was the only one that could put him back in his pen, many have tried and failed.

In my trance, I could see that things were going to be different for a while and that feeling in the pit of my stomach that you get when you're leaving someone behind, I felt worried and anxious, not so much for me but for Bob. I could see he was in the same place as me right now, I had stepped in and rescued him on many occasions and he had done the same to me, but this time we couldn't help each other, we had to hand the fight to each other.

I glanced up to the gallery to see what was peering down on us, it was Frank, Chris and Marty, front row their arms and shit tattoos poking through the bars that kept them from reaching us, backed by half of Teesside's good guys, there were no shitbag's up there, I guess the blue giro brigade were out spending the money they earned for dropping Bob and me in the courtroom, we will find ya, Bob will find ya.

I gave Frank half a smile and he threw one right back, Chris wanted to shout some verbal at the system and the bent coppers that have put us here, but he kept his cool, part of me wanted him to, but that wouldn't of helped.The local press were there waiting like vultures, drooling with their pens and notepads that tell more lies than congress, the place is silent as they read out the charges and their reasons to refuse us bail, "a danger to society my lord, a menace to Teesside my lord, a risk of fleeing the country your worship" our characters attacked like a village in Rwanda.Our legal team warned us this would happen, that didn't make it any easier, it was part of the plan. It all hurt every word, Bob was eager to shout "eh, al punch fuck out of every single one of ya" but he knew not to.

I looked across at him one more time and signalled for him to hold his head up and stand up straight to give the reporters something to chat shit about, we stood there waiting for the hammer to come down and echo through our souls, but we stood like soldiers to attention being inspected, smarter than them looking right at them, it was all happening like our people said it would, the hammer came down in slow motion, like a murder scene on a shit B movie, bang it hits the desk and we hear the words "take them down," I make eye contact with Bob who's glad it's over for now, I gave him a nod and he looks up at the bias judgmental magistrate and let's it out, "al find ya and al smash ya lass ya daft cunt" the gallery roared, the magistrate was confused "I beg your pardon" he mutters, "nothing your worship" smirks Bob, our pinstripe gave us a wink and a confident smile and whispers "ok you two we knew this would happen if you need anything call me."

Chris jumps out of seat, he can't contain himself anymore, "you will be back lads" then Frank stands up and as calm as you like shouts "stay cool kid." Hearing that gave me the strength to believe that this fight was ours Bob knew that too, I grabbed Bob one more time and gave him a man hug, whispering in his ear "we will be back kid don't worry," they pulled us apart like they were splitting up a fight, in a strange way they were, they just didn't realise it, we marched like guardsmen giving them fuck all and Bob, one last time throwing the threats at the sheriffs "If you shove me one more time, al bounce you every fucking wall in the room ya fat cunt," I laughed to myself, I knew I was gonna miss that, this was us accepting what was happening.

Rupert came to see us before we got shipped out and injected us one more time with confidence, defiance and the will that we needed. So as we are placed in the holding cell I stand and face the door legs apart neck in the back of my collar, in a show of arrogant defiance, my silhouette casting on the breezeblock behind me, the screw who has befriended me smiles and asks if I am ok one last time, I give him a wink and half of a smile "am sound kid," in the background I hear Bob's door shut and him shouting "who yatalking to, al punch fuck out of ya, when I get out of here I wanna grand off ya." Then it's my turn, the door swings and slams into place with the rattle of keys.

We are 25 and in deep water, but we had to remember we were good swimmers. If we can make it on our own here, when we come back, one thing's for sure.....we will be .... FUCKING UNSTOPPABLE.

You've read our life story up until 25... Look out for the final part of Bob & Dave's journey coming late in 2020... Keep following our Facebook page for further information.

THANKS –

Thanks to the other half of me Bob without whom this could not have been possible.

Jamie Boyle Author/Filmmaker who made this all happen.

Massive thanks to Warcry Publishing also.

Chris Everton who is the other secretpart of the famous duo and the real reason this story has come alive.

Big love to everyone involved and remember, if the boot fits then my job is done.

*"THE WHOLE OF BORO IS OURS,
AND EVERYTHING IN IT".*

Bob & Dave